MAN to MAN

Dr. Earl R. Henslin

Publishers Since 1798

THOMAS NELSON PUBLISHERS
Nashville

Published in Nashville, Tennessee, by Thomas Nelson, Inc., Publishers, and distributed in Canada by Word Communications, Ltd., Richmond, British Columbia, and in the United Kingdom by Word (UK), Ltd., Milton Keynes, England.

Scripture quotations are from The Holy Bible: NEW INTERNATIONAL VERSION, Copyright © 1978 by the New York International Bible Society. Used by permission of Zondervan Bible Publishers.

Scripture quotations noted NASB are from THE NEW AMERICAN STANDARD BILBE, Copyright © 1960, 1962, 1963, 1968, 1971, 1972, 1973, 1975, 1977 by The Lockman Foundation and are used by permission.

The names of persons and certain details of case histories described in this book have been changed to protect the author's clients. In certain cases, composit case histories have been constructed from actual cases.

Library of Congress Cataloging-in-Publication Data

Henslin, Earl R.
    Man to man / Earl R. Henslin.
       p.   cm.
    Includes bibliographical references.
    ISBN 0-8407-7724-8
    1. Fathers and sons. 2. Men—Psychology. I. Title.
HQ755.85.H457   1993
306.874′2—dc20
                                          93-15683
                                          CIP

Printed in the United States of America

1 2 3 4 5 6 7 — 99 98 97 96 95 94 93

CONTENTS ▲▲▲▲▲▲▲▲▲▲▲▲▲▲▲

Chapter 1
The Wound All Men Bear   *1*

Chapter 2
Understanding the Depth of the Father-Son Wound   *14*

Chapter 3
The Impact of the Father-Son Wound on Society   *32*

Chapter 4
The Impact of the Father Wound on a Man's Family Life   *47*

Chapter 5
The Impact of the Father Wound on a Man's Career   *64*

Chapter 6
The Impact of the Father Wound on a Man's Spiritual Life   *79*

Chapter 7
Masculine Growth Begins With Healing Relationships   *93*

Chapter 8
Building Bridges of Healing Between Father and Son   *106*

Chapter 9
Nurturing Masculine Growth for a Lifetime   *126*

Chapter 10
The Nurturing Role of Male Mentors   *141*

Chapter 11
The Healing Power of Male Friendships   *160*

Chapter 12
A Vision for the Church as a Healing Community   *188*

Appendices
Endnotes

I dedicate this book to my son, Ben.

I respect and admire the man you are becoming. I am sorry where I have failed you, and I pray that you may find a community of deeply feeling and spiritually committed Christian men to support and be with you on your journey through life. May God richly bless and guide you as you grow in your relationship with the Heavenly Father and in relationship with men here on earth. May He richly bless you as you develop the great gifts and abilities He has given you. I love you, Dad.

ACKNOWLEDGMENTS:

The list of men that follows symbolizes the message of this book. They are encouragers, supporters, and faithful friends who have been there with me through the tough times. I thank God for how He has used these men in my life. I could not be a man, husband, father, and therapist without them.

I thank my father for giving me the freedom to share whatever I needed to in this book. I pray that he finds the healing he needs for his father wound.

I thank my friend Vance Shepperson, Ph.D. for his faithfulness and consistency as a friend. I thank Will Hawkins, M.D., a faithful friend and mentor. I deeply respect his constant encouragement and consistency in prayer. I thank Bob Bartosch for allowing me to be a part of his life. I have a deep respect for the program of recovery he walks and for how God has worked through him and Pauline in the founding of Overcomers Outreach. I thank J. Keith Miller for his friendship and support. The example of how God has worked in his recovery is an inspiration to me. I also thank Dave Klimek, Ph.D. for his mentoring in my life during graduate school and for his faithful friendship today. I thank my pastor, Chuck Swindoll, for the consistency of his ministry and the model he presents of what happens when you let God work through you. I am thankful for his encouragement and interest in my work. I thank pastor Dave Carder, a strong friend and encourager during the journey of this men's book, and pastors Buck Buchanan, John Columbe, and Gary Richmond for their friendship and support. I especially thank Jim Dinsmore, who played a crucial role in encouraging me to go to graduate school.

I thank Amanda and Stephen Sorenson. Amanda you are a gifted writer. Your editing and polishing of this manuscript makes this book sound more like me than I am able to do. I also thank Terri Lopez, our office manager at Henslin and Associates, for her role in making this project possible. Thank you for the way God has used you to bring this book to print.

I thank Bill Henslin, who at age 86 provides a model of what a man can become as he ages. Bill is a man of warmth, love and grace. He is a man of acceptance who is not afraid to speak what is on his mind. He is a true patriarch of the Henslin family.

Most of all, I thank my wife Karen. Your love, encouragement, and belief in me means so much. None of this would be possible without you.

CHAPTER 1

The Wound All Men Bear

There's a saying in the South: "No man is a man until his father tells him he is." It means that someday when you're 30 or 40, grown up, this man—whom you respect and love and want to love you—puts his arms around you and says, "You know, you're a man now, and you don't have to do crazy things and get into fistfights and all that to defend the honor of men. You don't have to prove anything. You're a man, and I love you."[1]

After making this observation, actor Burt Reynolds continued to reveal more about his relationship with his father:

We never hugged, we never kissed, we never said, "I love you." No, we never cried.

So what happened was that I was desperately looking for someone who'd say, "You're grown up, and I approve and love you, and you don't have to do these things anymore." I was lost inside. I couldn't connect. I was incomplete. I didn't know then what I needed to know.[2]

In this surprisingly candid interview Reynolds clearly expresses the feelings of separation and woundedness that most men have suffered in their relationship with their fathers. Most men, no matter what their age, hunger for approval and love from other men. They hunger for a deep, emotional bond with their fathers. When men do not have that bond, when they do not receive that needed love and approval, they are deeply wounded.

In response to their unresolved father-son wound, many men do crazy things, such as denying their physical pain. Many men refuse to see a doctor when they hurt their backs or when they start having pains in their chests. They take incredible risks, suddenly becoming involved with daring pastimes such as motorcycle racing, sky diving, or bungee jumping. They see how close to the edge they can live. Some men work themselves to death, pushing themselves beyond fatigue and exhaustion until the next burst of adrenaline comes to keep them going for a few more hours.

These responses to inner woundedness damage men and those around them. In fact many of the desperate problems our society and its families must address today are rooted in the various responses men have to the woundedness they suffer in their relationships with their fathers. I realize this is a strong statement, but I am absolutely convinced that the father-son wound, while not the source of all male problems, plays a foundational role in men's issues. Furthermore, I believe that the key to activating masculine growth lies first within a man's relationship with his father and second within his relationships with other men. Subsequent chapters will give evidence of the pervasive and powerful impact of the father-son wound and present ways that men can heal from that wound.

The All-Important Relationship

It is no accident that the father-son wound has such a tremendous impact upon men. God created a fundamental need within all boys (and girls too) to be emotionally connected with their fathers. As one reads Scripture, which reveals the story of the family of Adam and Eve, it becomes evident that God created the father-son relationship to have great meaning and importance.

Jacob, for example, was willing to lie, manipulate, and deceive his father in order to gain his blessing (Genesis 27:1–29). Absalom, David's exiled son, so desperately wanted to be recognized by his father that he was willing to face death rather than live with rejection (2 Samuel 14:28–33). God sent a messenger to tell Eli how he had failed in his relationship with his two sons and to describe to Eli the consequences of his failure (1 Samuel 2:22–36). Throughout the book of Proverbs, Solomon praised his father's instruction.

Every aspect of a boy's developing personality reveals his need for a relationship with his father. A boy needs to experience not just an emotional connection, but a physical one as well. When a father wraps his strong arms around his infant son, the baby feels the physical security and emotional warmth of his father's embrace. As a little boy learns to walk and run, he needs a father who responds with empathy to the many cuts, bumps, and bruises he receives. When a boy is ready to ride a bike, he needs a father who can comfort him when he falls, but who can also urge him to take the risks of learning something new. An adolescent boy needs a father who deeply loves the boy's mother so that the boy will gain an understanding of what it means to be a husband. A boy needs a father who has an intimate relationship with God and can share spiritual reality from deep within his heart. A young man needs a father who can give of himself emotionally and physically without demanding that his son give anything in return. A father who can give of himself in this way gives his son the freedom to pursue his own direction and to discover the man God intends him to be. When a boy becomes a man, he needs a father who accepts him, loves him, and relates to him as a man.

This is the God-given well of need that lies within every boy. This is the well of need that a mother can never fill. She can only fill the need a boy has for a mother. God intended these deep needs to be met through the father-son relationship, the foundation from which a boy develops and matures into manhood. The father is the one who models what it means to both feel deeply and express those feelings. He models spiritual maturity and leadership; how to survive and provide for a family; and values such as integrity, obedience to God, purity, and compassion. God never intended fathers to do this job alone, however. God works through families and through the community of His people. The father-son relationship is the foundation; it starts things moving; yet if a boy is to develop his full masculine potential, he needs the input of a variety of other men. Becoming a man takes a lifetime. It takes a company of men from the boy's family and from the Christian community to nurture a boy from childhood into fully developed manhood.

The Father-Son Relationship Is Flawed

Although the father-son relationship is the most significant relationship in a man's life, it is not a perfect relationship. There are no perfect fathers and no perfect sons. Consequently, sons are wounded. Even the family histories recorded in Scripture give ample evidence that a wound exists between fathers and sons. Jacob, in his beautiful effort to express his love for his son Joseph, inflicted a deep wound upon Joseph's older brothers. A great emotional gulf existed between Isaac and Esau. The lives of David's sons, Amnon, Absalom, and Solomon, point toward deep wounds that never healed. The father of the prodigal son had tremendous love for both of his sons, but they suffered deep pain in their relationship with him.

Few fathers in Scripture and few fathers today have intentionally wounded their sons. Most fathers have done their best to care for their families and love their sons. They have worked hard to provide for their families and deserve honor and respect for the personal sacrifices they have made. Most fathers, however, have communicated their love primarily through material provision while their sons have yearned for fathers who could also express love physically and emotionally.

Most fathers have no idea that they need to be spiritual and emotional providers as well as material providers. They have difficulty bonding emotionally and spiritually with their sons because they have not experienced such bonding with their own fathers. Despite the fathers' earnest and loving efforts, their sons are wounded and do not feel their love.

As I lead workshops with men across the country, men in their seventies and eighties often express deep grief because they have lived their lives never really knowing, deep within their hearts, if their fathers truly loved or cared about them. Most men today, whether they are twenty-five, forty, or seventy, are basically starting out in the same place, with the same wound. They do not have the secure feeling of their fathers' deep, unfailing love for them.

When a Son Doesn't Feel Loved

It is hard for a son to feel secure in his father's love unless his father clearly and directly expresses his feelings through words and actions. A man might say "I love you" by giving his son a car, or he might express his love for a son by bailing him out of trouble. A boy's father might communicate his love by helping his son financially. These sincere expressions of love alone cannot make a son *feel* loved.

Consider the story of IBM founder Tom Watson and his son, Tom Watson, Jr. In *Father, Son, and Co.,* Tom Watson, Jr.[3] chronicles the rise of IBM from a company that made equipment to process time clock punch cards to a company that has led the world in computer development. This is also the story of a son who desperately wanted his father to say, "I love you, son. You're doing a great job."

Tom Watson, Jr. grew up with every social, financial, and educational advantage. His father was a role model of integrity, honesty, and caring for others. He was so fiercely loyal to his wife and children that he employed a male secretary so there would be no potential for accusations that he was unfaithful to his wife. Yet Tom Jr. had to share his father with the demands of an influential company that experienced periods of massive growth. His father traveled the country making sales and meeting with government officials. When sales declined, his father had to scramble to bring in business to avoid laying off employees. There are not enough hours in the day for a man to build an empire like IBM and be available for his kids too. So there was not much of a feeling connection between father and son.

As a young man Tom Jr. played the role of playboy and spoiled rich kid. When World War II began, he decided that he loved flying—something his father hated—and became a U.S. Air Force pilot. While serving as an aide and pilot for General Bradley, Tom Jr. soon discovered that his flight crew did not like or respect him because of his hard-driving, demanding ways. This realization initiated a change in young Watson— from a spoiled, egocentric, rich kid into a leader of men. He began affirming his men and responding to their emotional needs. They, in turn, became loyal to him and stood by him in thick and thin. On his own, far away from his father, Tom Jr. discovered what it took to be a leader.

Following the war, Tom struggled with the decision of whether to stay in the service or go to work with his father and eventually assume leadership of IBM. He discussed his indecision with General Bradley, confiding that he wondered at times if he had the ability to follow in his father's footsteps. The general not only expressed confidence that Tom could do the job, but added that he could not imagine Tom doing anything else. This was exactly the kind of assurance Tom needed to go back home to work with his father.

As I read this story, I could almost hear the voice of the little boy inside Tom Jr. crying out for the love, approval, and acceptance he desperately needed from his father. He needed to know that the man he respected and admired above all others truly believed in him. Every son needs to feel this kind of love from his father. Every man needs to feel this kind of love deep within his soul.

A father communicates this kind of love by being emotionally connected with his son. He forges this bond with his son when he shows that he cares about his child's feelings—by doing something as simple as hugging him when he cries. He forges an emotional bond when he takes his son seriously, perhaps by truly appreciating the scribbled piece of paper his three-year-old boy hands him. He creates a bond when he values his son's perceptions by listening carefully when he complains of an injustice among his playmates. He forges a bond when he joins in his son's experiences, such as going on a father-son camping trip. When that emotional bond between father and son is lacking, a son will feel lost, unloved, and will do the crazy things Burt Reynolds talked about earlier.

Discovering the Wound

The amazing thing is, most men either never realize that they have suffered a deep wound in their relationship with their fathers, or only discover this later in life. When men are in their early twenties, they have so much drive in the areas of athletics or women or work that they are not aware of what they really feel inside. Men remain unaware of their feelings because they generally are not expected to deal with them. Their feelings are not valued, probed, or challenged by other men, so they get away with ignoring their pain and confusion. Unless a man drinks or uses drugs too much, unless the emotional tension in the home is so great that the kids start acting crazy, unless his wife gets frustrated enough to insist on counseling or a divorce, or unless an event in life triggers those deep feelings, most men will not deal with their woundedness. I did not begin to realize that something was amiss in my life until I reached my early thirties. I would like to share how I started becoming aware of my father-son wound.

Things began changing for me when I met Bill Henslin, a distant cousin. I had recently moved from Minnesota to Southern California. I only met Bill because my great-uncle in Minnesota, whose name is also Bill Henslin, casually mentioned that I should look him up and that I would probably like him. Until that moment I did not know I had any relatives in Southern California. After I got settled, I followed up on my uncle's suggestion.

As I parked my car in front of Bill's house and began to walk up to the door, I felt nervous and excited. I did not quite know what to expect from this distant relative I had never met. I also felt a bit awed because I was about to meet, face to face, the son of one of my great-grandfather's brothers. This man had actually known my great-grandfather, Frank Henslin, who was born in 1852, 100 years earlier than I was. Bill was my link with the previous generations. He could tell me some of the legacies within my family.

Before I was halfway to the house, the door opened and an older man walked briskly toward me. My heart filled with warmth; here was an older man who was looking forward to meeting me! Straight and tall, he was rather handsome and distinguished looking. His broad smile radiated a life and energy that I was not used to seeing in the men of my family. I was struck by the way he resembled my grandfather, who had died when I was eighteen, and my great-uncle, who had always been kind to me.

As we approached each other, he reached out, grabbed my hand, and shook it warmly and gently. "I can tell you are a Henslin. You must be a fine young man," he said, smiling. "I am most happy to meet you."

Although this may seem like an ordinary greeting to you, it felt like a new experience for me. Here was a man who was meeting me for the first time and had already assumed the best about me. During our first personal interaction, which probably lasted only forty-five to fifty seconds, I felt more positive affirmation and direct expression of caring and warmth than I had felt from most of the other men in the family during my growing-up years.

When Bill Henslin greeted me, I felt an "I love you" with a depth that I had never felt before. Our meeting awakened an awareness of the deep sadness and grief that I carried inside. My relationship with him made me realize that I had missed out on something significant in my relationship with my father and in my relationships with other men in my family.

A few years later I heard Robert Bly speak. Bly is a poet and storyteller who has traveled the country for the past decade, speaking about men, their needs, masculinity, and the father-son wound. The observations he shared about men opened my eyes. As Bly spoke, I began to feel the depth of the sadness and grief within me. I began to realize that the emptiness deep in my heart was the wound I felt in my relationship with my father. This was a wound I had not only received from my father but also shared with him. I am sure my grandfather bore that wound as well. The men in my family had passed on that wound for generations, perhaps even for centuries.

The men in my family are hardworking, good men, but most of them are disconnected from their feelings. That is the norm for upper midwestern farm families like ours. We value hard work and consider it noble to bear, in stoic silence, whatever physical or emotional pain comes our way. Our unspoken rule is *men do not feel*. The men in our family know little about emotional expression. One rarely hears a hearty laugh or feels a warm hug from strong arms, or offers a spontaneous "I love you."

It is tragic that sons should suffer such loss and woundedness from fathers who truly love them, but it happens. I know my father loved me. I know he cared. He worked hard, sacrificed for his family, and was a good provider, but he did not know how to help me *feel* loved. I also know that my father did not feel loved by his father. He never received affirmation from his father, and I doubt that he ever felt the warmth and comfort of a loving hug from his father. My father was unable to give what he had never received himself. He didn't have a clue about how to reach out to me emotionally because no one had ever reached out to him.

Most men have suffered the same wound as the men in my family. They have never known what it feels like to be emotionally connected to their fathers. They have never known if their fathers think they are diligent students, good athletes, successful businessmen, or fine family men. They have never known if their fathers accept them and consider them worthy of respect or admiration.

The Emptiness Within

The saddest part of this whole situation is that most fathers have these good feelings about their sons. Most fathers respect their sons and are proud of their accomplishments but just do not know how to share those feelings. So most men, as Burt Reynolds has eloquently described, feel lost, disconnected, and incomplete. They feel a deep sadness because they are never really sure how their fathers feel about them.

Today that emptiness is greater than ever before because so many sons have a severely limited amount of time with their fathers. In many cases the time sons do have with their fathers can in no way be called "quality time." Robert Bly states, "The average father in the United States talks to his son less than 10 minutes a day. And that talk may be talk from a distance, such as 'Is your room cleaned up?' or 'Are you on drugs?'"[4]

At least in agricultural times, sons had the experience of working side by side with their fathers. Although they may not have received much direct expression of love from them, they at least had the opportunity to be in their fathers' presence for a number of hours each day. For the past five or six decades maturing boys have rarely had such intimate, daily contact with their fathers. Many fathers work in offices or factories that may be an hour or two away from home. Others are on the road Monday through Friday and struggle to fit a week's worth of yard work, family time, and bill paying into a weekend. Still others may work in another part of the world for weeks or even months at a time, sharing only a few phone calls or letters with their families. It is difficult for a father to have an intimate, emotional relationship with his son under such circumstances, yet the son's need for emotional bonding with his father has not lessened. The wound created by the lack of such a relationship is devastating.

As a result of this tremendous emotional loss, most men spend their lives trying to do two things: to prove themselves to their fathers and to fill the emptiness in their souls. This twofold need is often the dominant force in a man's life, leading to incredible dysfunction that threatens every aspect of his life.

Proving One's Worth to Dad

Every boy yearns to be sought out by his father. When a boy lacks this emotional connection, his natural response is to try to do something that will cause his father to demonstrate his love for him, something that will create an emotional bond between them. Different boys try different behaviors. One boy will become an overachiever. *Maybe if I do well enough in school or make the basketball team,* the boy reasons, *Dad will think I'm special.* Another boy will cause trouble at home or at school until he gains his father's attention. Regardless of the outward behavior, the motivation is the same—to be emotionally connected or close to the father.

When I was young, for example, I excelled in music and sports. In ninth grade I played first trumpet in the senior band, and by tenth grade I played on the varsity basketball team.

Every time I did well, I wanted my dad to give me a big hug and tell me so, but the hug never came.

As I grew older, I became increasingly depressed. I rarely smiled and I spent a lot of time alone because it seemed easier to isolate myself when I felt hurt. I needed my father to recognize my pain, reach out to me, and make an emotional connection that would heal some of the pain I felt. His inability to respond to my feelings only fueled my depression.

Every boy truly believes that he can do something to make that emotional connection with his father. He believes that if he does just the right thing, his father will approve of him and he will have earned his father's affection. Unfortunately this is not true. The father, not the son, is the one who must build the emotional bridge between father and son. But the myth persists, and within many adult men there is a little boy who is still trying to prove himself to his dad.

For example, Tom Watson, Jr. struggled well into his adult life to earn his father's approval. However, no amount of performance on the son's part can produce the emotional bonding he seeks. That connection begins only when the father reaches out to his son. If this never happens, the boy must wait until he is well into adulthood—and his own process of healing—to attempt to make an emotional connection with his father (see Chapter 8).

Filling the Emptiness Inside

In the absence of this emotional bond, a man will do almost anything to fill the aching sense of loss he feels inside. Some men resort to angry, destructive behaviors. Some bury their pain in a variety of addictions—work, alcohol, sex, food, or drugs. Some men immerse themselves in relentless religious activity, serving on church boards and committees but rarely touching people's hearts. Some men put all of their feeling and passion into their yards, meticulously weeding and nurturing them but neglecting to nurture themselves or their families.

Occasionally a man will be fortunate enough to try to fill that emptiness in positive ways, through deep relationships with other men. For example, when I met Bill Henslin and first consciously felt the tremendous loss and overwhelming grief related to my relationship with my father, I realized that I had been seeking out surrogate fathers for years. In my late teens, without really knowing what I was doing, I had recognized the value of men and sought out deep relationships with them. I had searched for male friends who could touch the needs of the hurting little boy inside me—the child who, because of his wounded relationship with his father, felt he was too young for the job and never adequate to meet the challenge—and encourage me to grow in the world of men. I had also realized that finding a man I could trust was one of the most valuable and precious things in the world.

Without intending to, I had begun to heal from the wounds of my father-son relationship. In the absence of an emotional bridge with my father, I had discovered that deep relationships with other men were the next best thing. I was fortunate, indeed, to have discovered the same thing David found in his relationship with Jonathan. When David mourned Jonathan's death, he said: "I grieve for you, Jonathan my brother; you were very dear to me. Your love for me was wonderful, more wonderful than that of women" (2 Samuel 1:26).

Chapter 2

Understanding the Depth of the Father-Son Wound

No one can touch the depth of a son's soul the way his father can. No one else can touch a son's feelings, shape his self-image, or move his spirit as his father does. Despite this inherent intimacy, the emotional connection between father and son does not automatically happen. The father has to make it happen.

The sad truth is, most fathers do not even know they have a God-given responsibility to build an emotional bridge to their sons, much less how to go about doing it. They have no idea that God intends their sons to discover their feelings and learn how to manage those feelings through their influence. They do not know that God intends their sons to develop a healthy attitude toward women, to learn to respect and value the opposite sex, through their influence. They are unaware that God intends their sons to learn to care for themselves and others through their influence. They do not know that their sons form values and develop principles for living by observing their example in everyday life.

Since most fathers are unaware of the importance of their role, and therefore are unable to make a conscious effort to fulfill it, their sons are deeply wounded. This damage occurs not because fathers want to harm their sons, but because fathers basically have been unaware of the impact they have on their son's lives. To understand more about the nature and depth of the father-son wound, let us look at some of the many ways in which it can occur.

A Son Is Wounded When His Father Doesn't Respond to His Emotions

Although most men learn to deny their emotions, God created men with the ability to experience a variety of deep feelings. Young boys who haven't learned to deny their feelings express them freely, hungering for a heartfelt response. But instead of a supportive response, most boys receive rejection or a reaction from their fathers. This is deeply wounding.

To illustrate, suppose a little boy falls down, hurts himself, and begins to cry. A father's emotional *response* would be to put his arms around the boy, to let him know he is safe, and to comfort him. Such assurance lets the boy know that the hurt is real and that the father understands what it is like to feel pain. A father's emotional *reaction,* on the other hand, would be to say, "What are you whimpering about? That's only a scratch!" Such a reaction causes fear in the little boy. His body tenses, he feels shamed, he begins to program himself to ignore pain, and—most important—he decides never to express his pain again. The boy begins to realize that his father does not seem to have any pain, so he should not either.

Unfortunately, the little boy may then grow up to be a man who ignores his pain until it becomes so severe he can no longer function. He may go through life denying the pain in his stomach or chest until he has a bleeding ulcer or needs a triple bypass. At that point it will take radical spiritual, medical, and psychological intervention to reverse the damage that has been done.

Or, the little boy may discover that eating numbs his

emotional pain. Perhaps he will learn that after he eats a dozen cookies, a half-gallon of ice cream, or a bag of chips, his misery goes away. As he grows older, that discovery may lead to compulsive eating in which food, rather than God and other men, becomes his primary source of support. He may go through life weighing twenty, fifty, even a hundred pounds more than he should. Being overweight will lead to serious physical problems.

Or, when a boy is a bit older, he may discover that alcohol numbs his inner pain in a way nothing else does. He may feel that if he has enough alcohol, he can put the pain behind him and get on with his life. Or perhaps the adolescent boy discovers that masturbating or viewing pornographic material enables him to feel better for a time. All of these efforts to deaden his inner pain can lead a young man into compulsive, uncontrollable activities that will destroy his life.

As you can see, a little boy who experiences his father's emotional reaction rather than an empathetic response to his needs may suffer for a lifetime. Regrettably, other men—uncles, grandfathers, coaches, pastors, and teachers—may reinforce the father's message of emotional disapproval and rejection. Often the older men with whom the little boy has contact give him the same message: *Big boys don't cry. What happens to you really doesn't hurt.*

Of course there is a time and place to deny pain in order to sacrifice for a larger goal, and as boys become men they need to learn when this is appropriate. An example of appropriate denial of pain would be the training a man endures in boot camp. In combat conditions, mental alertness and an ability to respond as one has been trained—regardless of personal needs and inner feelings—is necessary. To respond otherwise could result in death for the individual and others who depend on him.

For a boy growing into manhood, however, it is devastating to deny pain as a way of life. When that happens, the boy learns to handle his pain by pushing through it. This attitude may seem courageous and noble, but it usually renders him unable to discern his inner feelings or to respond to the feelings of others, even the feelings of loved ones.

Don, a friend of mine, was such a man. He grew up with an emotionally reactive father. Life was not easy on their small midwestern farm. Side by side, father and son put in twelve- to fourteen-hour days. His father's only concession to physical exhaustion was his customary, three-hour Sunday afternoon nap, which refreshed him only enough to begin work again on Monday morning. No matter what task Don was assigned, he had to complete it perfectly. No excuses were allowed for physical limitations or for slow or flawed work.

For Don, entering the military after high school was a relief. Basic training was like working part time in comparison to the way he had worked on the farm. The training he had received at home more than prepared him for the emotional rigors of military life. As a little boy he had learned to survive by extreme emotional denial. As an adult, he was so emotionally detached that he rarely felt the hurt that lingered deep inside.

While in the service, Don finally discovered a source of comfort: alcohol. It not only made him feel better, it gave him a feeling of camaraderie, a sense of belonging with the other men in his unit. It was consoling to go out on leave and drink and laugh with other men. Once out of the service, the only time Don found similar camaraderie was when he stopped with his friends for a drink or two after work. But Don's wife objected to his after-work drinking, and when he was promoted to management, his former buddies no longer invited him to join them.

At this point in his life, liquor became Don's best friend and most constant companion. As his alcoholism progressed, he became increasingly distant and argumentative with his wife. Even though he was proud of his sons, he did not really know how to have fun with them or be close to them. It seemed that Don's life was limited to long hours of work, a few brief conversations over the back fence with his neighbor, and drinking—

something he did on evenings and weekends when he was alone at home or while puttering around the garage or yard.

Don was a good man. He provided well for his wife and children, but by the time he reached his early fifties, his body was worn out. His arteries could only carry about 20 to 25 percent of the blood his body needed, and he suffered a heart attack. Too much food, work, and alcohol, combined with too little exercise, too few close relationships with family and friends, and too distant a relationship with God, had taken their toll. Only an emergency triple bypass and help for his alcoholism gave him a second chance to face the emptiness he felt inside. Only life-threatening circumstances opened Don's eyes to the fact that his father's inability to understand and respond to his feelings had set him up to become a man just like his father—one who knew how to work and drink but had no idea how to be a responsive, loving friend, husband, and father.

A Son Is Wounded When His Father Is Absent

Every boy needs his father's active involvement in his life; yet many sons suffer abandonment in their relationship with their fathers. Some fathers intentionally abandon their families—a tremendously deep hurt for a boy to bear. Other fathers, while they have not abandoned their families, are frequently not at home. Still others are physically present but emotionally absent. The sons of these fathers suffer feelings of abandonment in the father-son relationship.

Obviously, the son whose father has completely abandoned the family suffers the deepest wound. In some cases, the son was so young when the abandonment occurred that he has no memory of ever seeing his father. In others, a son has never even known his father's name; he doesn't have a clue about his father's identity and would not know him if he met him face to face.

These sons have a huge void, an empty hole, inside. They have never been able to observe their fathers to see what it means to be a man, a husband, or a father. Often the extended family of these boys is so fragmented that they have never seen these roles modeled by a responsible man. Most of their learning about life has come through their peers rather than through relationships with their fathers, uncles, or grandfathers.

These sons also feel great shame. Often they wonder, *What's wrong with me that my dad didn't stick around? Why doesn't he care enough about me to be here? What did I do to make him go away? Why doesn't he even want to know who I am?* Sometimes the father-son wound in these boys is so deep that they never have a meaningful relationship with any man.

Intentional, permanent abandonment is a tragedy of incredible magnitude, but much lesser degrees of abandonment leave great wounds too. Many fathers work ten to fifteen hours a day to build up their businesses or to climb the corporate ladder. A father who is doing this is absent during most of his son's waking hours, particularly when the son is young. Even when the father is home, he is often so tired and emotionally drained that he can do little to build an emotional bridge to his son. The father does not have the time to play with him, the sensitivity to listen to him, or the energy to share his strength, convictions, and values with him.

To the son, this physical and emotional absence feels like abandonment. The son may seek out other sources—television, a favorite coach, a gang—to find what is missing in his relationship with his father. The son also feels a certain amount of shame because he interprets his father's absence to be the result of his inadequacy or his failure to please him. These feelings may also result when a father is emotionally absent due to alcoholism, drug use, or other addictions.

Another type of abandonment occurs when a father has an extramarital affair. When a man has an affair, he makes a clear emotional statement that another relationship is more important than his relationship with his family, more important than his relationship with his son. A son is devastated, and often outraged, when his father has an affair. Wounded and shamed, the son usually concludes, *I don't mean anything to you!*

The father-son wound deepens if the father divorces and remarries, particularly if his new wife has children who live with them. The son then sees that his father cares about children who are not even his, while he only gets to see his father on weekends or during school vacations. This wound leads to jealousy and rivalry between stepchildren, and deeper distrust and feelings of shame between father and son.

A Son Is Wounded When His Father Is Physically Abusive

A boy is greatly wounded when his father is physically abusive. Even in Christian homes, such abuse is not as uncommon as we would like to think. In fact, the wave of physical abuse in our society is so great that there is a movement to eliminate all corporal punishment. Physical abuse often occurs while parents are disciplining their children. A father may become abusive when he loses control while punishing his son for some wrongdoing, or he may use too harsh or severe a physical punishment. Sadly, a number of abusive Christian fathers believe they are following a biblical model of authority when they dole out liberal doses of physical punishment.

Please do not misunderstand me. I in no way recommend liberal or permissive parenting. I am all for parents who set strong limits and boundaries for their children. I fully support confrontation of sinful behavior. However, I have counseled too many Christian adults who, under the name of biblical discipline, suffered physical abuse at the hands of their parents. I have counseled young men who struggle with rage, depression, and various addictions in their attempts to silence the pain of abuse they carry deep inside. I have seen adult men cry when they remember the feelings of shame and woundedness they suffered from their father's "discipline." True biblical discipline does not leave such deep woundedness in its wake.

An even greater tragedy is that abuse by Christian fathers

leaves behind far more than bruises and shame. Although a boy may learn to avoid a particular behavior for which he is punished, he may also be terribly confused about his relationship with his parents and with God. A boy who has been physically abused by his father will often view God as being punitive too. He may feel that if he fails to live perfectly in every way, God will become violently angry with him—as if God is just waiting for an excuse to pour His wrath and judgment down upon him.

A Son Is Wounded When His Father Reacts With Rage or Shame

Rage is a type of emotional abuse. The damage suffered through a father's emotional abuse is similar to that which results from his physical abuse. In both emotional and physical abuse, a boy feels shame and emotionally distances himself from his father. A boy also learns to deny his feelings, often engaging in whatever behaviors seem to insulate him from his emotional pain.

Some fathers emotionally abuse their sons by reacting with rage to their son's mistakes. For instance, a boy may accidently break a window while playing ball in the backyard with his friends. If his father responds with rage and yells at him in front of his friends, his father is wounding the son. The boy may channel the wound from his father's rage into becoming a great baseball player or he may be afraid to risk anything. Deep inside the boy will live with the fear that if he makes a mistake and does not do things just right, something bad will happen to him.

It is not uncommon for fathers to react to their sons in this abusive way. We even see examples of this type of behavior in Scripture. Saul, for instance, raged at his son, Jonathan, when Jonathan foiled Saul's plan to murder David. Notice the rage and shame in the interaction between father and son:

> . . . Then Saul said to his son Jonathan, "Why hasn't

the son of Jesse come to the meal, either yesterday or today?"

Jonathan answered, "David earnestly asked me for permission to go to Bethlehem. He said, 'Let me go, because our family is observing a sacrifice in the town and my brother has ordered me to be there. If I have found favor in your eyes, let me get away to see my brothers.' That is why he has not come to the king's table."

Saul's anger flared up at Jonathan and he said to him, "You son of a perverse and rebellious woman! Don't I know that you have sided with the son of Jesse to your own shame and to the shame of the mother who bore you? As long as the son of Jesse lives on this earth, neither you nor your kingdom will be established. Now send and bring him to me, for he must die!"

"Why should he be put to death? What has he done?" Jonathan asked his father. But Saul hurled his spear at him to kill him. Then Jonathan knew that his father intended to kill David.

Jonathan got up from the table in fierce anger. . . .

1 Samuel 20:27–34

This is not your normal dinnertime conversation. Saul rages at Jonathan, publicly humiliates him, insults him, taunts him, and even tries to kill him. Although Scripture doesn't tell us how this interaction affected Jonathan's heart, you can be sure it affected him deeply. Rage always shames a son, and shame is a deep wound.

An old Jewish proverb says that publicly shaming a man is like shedding his blood. Shame is one of the deep wounds men receive from their fathers, from society, and from the Christian community. Many men have deep layers of shame that keep them from feeling their emotions.

Shame not only occurs when a father rages at his son, but during much of the daily interaction between father and son. A son is shamed when his father says, "Oh, grow up! Big boys don't cry. That's nothing to cry about!" A son is humiliated if his father is obviously drunk when the boy's friends come to visit. When a father promises to be at a ball game and does not show up, the son's shame grows deeper. A son is shamed if his father physically or sexually abuses him. A father who notices his son's lack of perfection or failures more than his accomplishments also dumps a load of shame onto him. A father is shaming when he expects his son to know how to do a task, such as changing the oil or mowing the lawn, without proper instruction.

When a son is blasted with his father's rage or shame, his only option is to do what Jonathan did—to leave. When a father abuses his son in this manner, any emotional bridge that may have existed between them is destroyed. There is no longer any way the son can talk reasonably with his father. If the son is unable to leave his father physically, as Jonathan did, he will cut himself off from his father emotionally.

A Son Is Wounded When His Father Is Sexually Abusive

Sexual abuse is one of the deepest wounds a boy can suffer. Estimates indicate that one out of every six men has been sexually abused, but I believe those figures are low because sexual abuse is so difficult for men to talk about. Although all such abuse is damaging, it is most damaging when a boy's father has been the abuser.

Sexual abuse by the father is one of the most fragmenting things that can happen to a boy. It is a violation of a boy's whole being—emotionally, spiritually, and physically. It literally tears a boy apart, leaving him with a lifelong sense of shame and the belief that he is a bad person. Often an abusive father will tell a boy that the sexual abuse is well-deserved punishment for something the boy has done. Many times such abuse is so traumatic that a boy completely blocks out its memory.

Sexual abuse by the father has a lifelong impact on a boy

because the father plays the predominant role in shaping his son's view of sexuality. Sexual abuse from the father creates confusion in the boy's sexual orientation. The father's abuse makes all men appear to be dangerous, but simultaneously creates a deep attraction for close relationships with other men—a result of the boy's hunger for his father's true affection. It is not uncommon for a boy who has been sexually abused by his father to become a homosexual. Other men who have been sexually abused may turn toward pornography, and other forms of sexual addiction. Even if he pursues heterosexual relationships, he often feels physically inadequate and has difficulty communicating within those relationships.

Obviously, a father who makes inappropriate sexual advances toward his son or forces his son to participate in deviant sexual acts wounds and shames his son deeply. Covert forms of sexual abuse leave deep wounds too. If a father brings pornography into the home, he exposes his son to a distorted view of sexuality and women. A father who makes disrespectful sexual comments about women, such as commenting about the size of a woman's breasts or referring to a woman as a whore or slut, communicates a distorted view of masculine sexuality to his son. A father who looks at all women in a sexual way also influences his son's view of masculinity and femininity. A father who is passive or silent about sexuality also wounds his son because he has abandoned his responsibility to nurture his son's developing sexuality. His son then learns about sexuality from friends, television, and whatever he might read, which is not the way God intended a young man to develop his sexual identity.

A Son Is Wounded When There Is Covert Incest in the Home

God designed the family to operate so that the primary relationship exists between the husband and wife. But in a troubled marriage, this often does not happen. When the spiritual and emotional bond between husband and wife is broken, the primary relationships often exist between child(ren) and parent(s). When this kind of relationship exists between child and parent rather than husband and wife, we call it covert incest. As we will see, covert incest devastates the father-son relationship. It is perhaps one of the most common forms of emotional and sexual abuse today.

Kenneth Adams aptly describes the devastating impact of covert incest:

> *Covert incest* occurs when a child becomes the object of a parent's affection, love, passion and preoccupation. The parent, motivated by the loneliness and emptiness created by a chronically troubled marriage or relationship, makes the child a surrogate partner. The boundary between caring and incestuous love is crossed when the relationship with the child exists to meet the needs of the parent rather than those of the child. As the deterioration in the marriage progresses, the dependency on the child grows and the opposite-sex parent's response to the child becomes increasingly characterized by desperation, jealousy, and a disregard for personal boundaries. The child becomes an object to be manipulated and used so the parent can avoid the pain and reality of a troubled marriage.
>
> The child feels used and trapped, the same feelings overt incest victims experience. Attempts at play, autonomy and friendship render the child guilt-ridden and lonely, never able to feel okay about his or her needs. Over time, the child becomes preoccupied with the parent's needs and feels protective and concerned. A psychological marriage between parent and child results. The child becomes the parent's surrogate spouse.
>
> . . . An important difference between overt and covert incest is that, while the overt victim feels abused, the covert victim feels idealized and privileged. Yet underneath the thin mask of feeling special and privileged rests the same trauma of the overt victim: rage, anger, shame and guilt. . . . The adult covert incest victim remains stuck in a

pattern of living aimed at keeping the special relationships going with the opposite-sex parent. It is a pattern of always trying to please Mommy or Daddy.[1]

The symptoms of covert incest are not difficult to recognize. Most of them apply to adult children as well as younger children:

- The parent looks toward the child for emotional support that is not provided by the spouse.
- The child is the primary source of the parent's emotional support.
- The parent would rather spend time with the child than with the spouse.
- The parent shares angry, critical feelings with the child concerning the spouse.
- The parent's happiness rises and falls with the child's accomplishments.
- The parent becomes resentful or jealous of the child's happiness or accomplishments.
- The child is afraid or worried that the parent's marriage will fail unless he or she supports the parents.
- The child worries about what might happen if he or she is not available to meet the parent's needs.
- The married child is closer and more emotionally supportive of his or her parent than his or her spouse.
- The child feels that he or she exists for the parent's needs. When the parent does not reciprocate, the child feels used or manipulated.
- The parent provides emotional support and encouragement for the child, but does not provide such support for the spouse.

The Bible provides a remarkable example of the impact covert incest can have on a family, particularly its impact on the father-son relationship. The story begins in Genesis 25, and concerns the relationship of Isaac and Rebekah and their twin sons, Jacob and Esau.

From Scripture's first mention of this family, we see conflict among its members. Even before birth, the twins struggled against each other (Genesis 25:22–25). As the boys matured, each parent chose a favorite: "Esau became a skillful hunter, a man of the open country, while Jacob was a quiet man, staying among the tents. Isaac, who had a taste for wild game, loved Esau, but Rebekah loved Jacob" (Genesis 25:27–28). As the firstborn, Esau had the right to receive the primary blessing from this father. But Scripture says Esau "despised his birthright" (Genesis 25:34), and when he returned home hungry from a futile hunting trip, sold his birthright to his younger brother in exchange for stew (Genesis 25:29–34). Notice that Jacob did not just take Esau's word for the exchange: "But Jacob said, 'Swear to me first.' So he swore an oath to him, selling his birthright to Jacob" (Genesis 25:33).

Betrayal and a lack of trust among family members was not just evident in the relationship between the brothers. In Genesis 26:1-10, we learn that Isaac put Rebekah at great personal risk in order to save his own neck. During a time of famine, God had promised to protect and bless Isaac and his descendants, and specifically told him where to live (vv. 2–6). However, "When the men of that place asked him about his wife, he said, 'She is my sister,' because he was afraid to say, 'She is my wife.' He thought, 'The men of this place might kill me on account of Rebekah, because she is beautiful'" (v. 7). Later, the king was horrified to learn what Isaac had done and said, "What is this you have done to us? One of the men might well have slept with your wife, and you would have brought guilt upon us" (v. 10).

There is no doubt that Isaac's self-protective lie put Rebekah at great physical, emotional, and spiritual risk. Even though he received a direct promise from God that he would be safe, he rejected the opportunity to live by faith. Instead, he responded in fear and betrayed his wife. I find it interesting that on two different occasions, when faced with similar circumstances, Isaac's father, Abraham, also claimed that his wife was his sister (see Genesis 12:10–20; 20:1–16). Tragically, when we examine the history of many families, we often see the same problems occur generation after generation. It takes courage to take steps that no man in your family has taken before. Isaac was apparently unable to take that courageous step of faith and, like his father, chose to put his wife at great personal risk.

It is my opinion that Isaac's actions created a wound in his relationship with Rebekah that never healed. I also believe that wound contributed greatly to the covert incest that eventually shattered the family and led to tremendous wounds in the father-son relationships. Let us see how the wound Rebekah felt in her marital relationship was played out through her children many years later.

When Isaac was old and his eyes were so weak that he could no longer see, he called for Esau his older son and said to him, "My son."
"Here I am," he answered.
Isaac said, "I am now an old man and don't know the day of my death. Now then, get your weapons—your quiver and bow—and go out to the open country to hunt some wild game for me. Prepare me the kind of tasty food I like and bring it to me to eat, so that I may give you my blessing before I die."

Genesis 27: 1–4

Now Rebekah was listening as Isaac spoke to his son Esau. When Esau left for the open country to hunt game and bring it back, Rebekah said to her son Jacob:

Look, I overheard your father say to your brother Esau, "Bring me some game and prepare me some tasty food to

eat, so that I may give you my blessing in the presence of
the Lord before I die." Now, my son, listen carefully and do
what I tell you: Go out to the flock and bring me two
choice young goats, so I can prepare some tasty food for
your father, just the way he likes it. Then take it to your father to eat, so that he may give you his blessing before he dies.

Genesis 27:6–10

Jacob expressed concern about being caught in such deception, but his mother assured him she would prepare the food
and disguise him in such a way that Isaac would never know
he was blessing Jacob rather than Esau. When Isaac ques-
tioned whether or not the son before him truly was Esau, Jacob
lied and said he was. Together, Jacob and Rebekah succeeded
in deceiving Isaac (see Genesis 27:11–29).

The fact that Rebekah would even think of such deception
indicates that the spiritual and emotional bond between husband and wife had been broken. That Jacob would even consider her plot indicates a strong emotional bond between
mother and son. Jacob had begun to view his father through
his mother's eyes. The father-son relationship was clearly
damaged. The fact that Jacob could openly lie to his father
further indicates his lack of respect for him. But the story is
not over yet:

After Isaac finished blessing him and Jacob had
scarcely left his father's presence, his brother Esau came in
from hunting. He too prepared some tasty food and
brought it to his father. Then he said to him, "My father,
sit up and eat some of my game, so that you may give me
your blessing."

His father Isaac asked him, "Who are you?"

"I am your son," he answered, "your firstborn, Esau."

Isaac trembled violently and said, "Who was it, then,
that hunted game and brought it to me? I ate it just before
you came and I blessed him—and indeed he will be
blessed!"

29

When Esau heard his father's words, he burst out with a loud and bitter cry and said to his father, "Bless me—me too, my father!"

But he said, "Your brother came deceitfully and took your blessing."

Esau said, "Isn't he rightly named Jacob? He has deceived me these two times: He took my birthright, and now he's taken my blessing!" Then he asked, "Haven't you reserved any blessing for me?"

Isaac answered Esau, "I have made him lord over you and have made all his relatives his servants, and I have sustained him with grain and new wine. So what can I possibly do for you, my son?"

Esau said to his father, "Do you have only one blessing, my father? Bless me too, my father!" Then Esau wept aloud.

Genesis 27:30–38

Can you feel the deep pain both Isaac and Esau are suffering as they realize what Rebekah and her accomplice Jacob have taken from them?

Isaac realizes that he has been betrayed, that his own son has lied to him. He is so enraged by what has happened that he is shaking. Perhaps he suspects that Rebekah had something to do with these events—that she finally got back at him for her deep-seated anger about what he had done to her years earlier.

Esau is devastated. He has been waiting his whole life for the day when his father would give him his blessing. To be blessed by his father is a very special moment in a man's life. The father's blessing conveys his unchangeable approval and acceptance of his son as a man; yet Esau has been robbed of the most meaningful event in his life. Feeling the loss, he repeatedly asks his father for a blessing—any blessing. His anguished cry of deep sadness and loss is undeniable.

Jacob, on the other hand, has accomplished his mother's wishes and received the blessing he wanted, but not without paying a tremendous price. Whatever relationship he had with his brother is now shattered and will remain that way for much of his life. Even more important, by deceiving his father, Jacob loses the benefit of a relationship with him. By stealing his father's blessing for Esau, Jacob misses out on whatever experiences or blessing his father would have shared with him. Although Jacob does not articulate his loss as dramatically as Esau, it is nonetheless painful.

All sons need the blessing of a deep and meaningful relationship with their fathers. Whether they are grandsons of the patriarch Abraham, sons of farmers, or sons of the founders of worldwide corporations, all boys need to be emotionally connected with their fathers. All boys need the heartfelt love and intimate involvement of their fathers if they are to fully grow into manhood. When men do not receive this, they bear a father-son wound that affects every aspect of their lives. When enough men are wounded in this way, the whole society changes, which is what we will examine in the following chapter.

Chapter **3**
▲▲▲▲▲▲▲▲▲▲▲

The Impact of the Father-Son Wound on Society

When a true emotional bonding occurs between father and son, the son gains a solid personal foundation that will last a lifetime. He gains a sense of his personal identity, acquires his core values, develops solid convictions, attains a sense of purpose, and discovers a masculine strength he can draw upon during difficult times. The tragedy of our time is that most men have not experienced this fundamental emotional bond in their relationship with their fathers. This loss of masculine intimacy has yielded tragic results.

Young men who are in their late teens and twenties today seem overwhelmed and unable to discover direction and purpose in their lives. This is, in some ways, a normal developmental stage. The young men I counsel, however, seem to hunger for guidance and direction from an older man. Unfortunately, most of these young men lack relationships with fathers, grandfathers, uncles, or older churchmen to whom they can turn for insight and advice.

Many young men have another problem stemming from the lack of an older man's influence in their lives: they have not developed a good work ethic. Many of them do not understand the concept of paying one's dues in the workplace, of starting at the bottom and working toward the top. They do not understand what it means to take on responsibility and carry a job through to completion, so when the job gets too hard or uncomfortable, they want to bail out.

Perhaps the most devastating problem of all is that so many young men today lack a basic foundation of moral character. Many cannot imagine waiting until marriage to have sex or having a lifelong monogamous relationship. For many young men, sex is like holding hands was thirty years ago—almost that casual. The moral values that men in our society once had have not been passed down to today's young men.

The loss of masculine intimacy also affects men who are in their thirties and forties. When men reach the difficult time of midlife, they reach deep inside to draw upon the inner resources that they hope will carry them through. Most men find nothing but emptiness. They have no inner strength upon which to draw. They have no unshakable values or convictions. They have no experience of masculine closeness or feeling of masculine support. And most have no close relationships with older men to whom they can turn for wisdom and from whom they can muster courage and strength.

Perhaps the greatest symptom of this loss of masculine connection is the lack of commitment that men, particularly those in midlife, seem to have to family and marriage. It seems all too easy for men today to betray their marriages and have an affair, to abandon their marriages and pursue the illusion of a more satisfying relationship.

Even the older men in society who have survived many difficulties in life bear the painful consequences of broken father-son relationships. They do not seem to recognize the influence, power, and responsibility they have. They do not seem to understand that they need to affirm and support younger men, to take their leadership role in the church and community seriously. Many older men seem content to golf, fish, and bowl, when they have much of value to offer society.

The State of Men Today

The loss of masculine intimacy yields tragic results, not only in the lives of individual men but in society at large. Examples of the disintegration of basic values in our society abound. The wound in father-son relationships has contributed to the disintegration of the family, to the demise of Christian influence in our culture, to the loss of confidence in those who hold leadership positions. It has contributed to the moral vacuum evidenced by rioting in our cities, scandals among our financial institutions, ever-increasing numbers of abortions, and a lack of integrity among our elected officials.

The changes that have taken place in society are so dramatic that James Patterson and Peter Kim, authors of *The Day America Told the Truth: What People Really Believe About Everything That Really Matters*[1], have compiled a new set of "commandments" by which they believe American society now lives. They have concluded that no moral consensus exists in America today. Instead, individuals make up their own moral code. Patterson and Kim base the commandments they have compiled on numerous surveys they have conducted among men and women of all ages.

Ten Commandments for the 1990s

1. I don't see the point of observing the Sabbath (77 percent).
2. I will steal from those who won't really miss it (74 percent).
3. I will lie when it suits me, so long as it does not cause any real damage (64 percent).
4. I will drink and drive if I feel that I can handle it. I know my limit (56 percent).

5. I will cheat on my spouse—after all, given the chance, he or she will do the same (53 percent).
6. I will procrastinate at work and do absolutely nothing about one full day in every five. It is standard operating procedure (50 percent).
7. I will use recreational drugs (41 percent).
8. I will cheat on my taxes—to a point (30 percent).
9. I will put my lover at risk of disease. I sleep around a bit, but who doesn't (31 percent).
10. Technically, I may have committed date rape, but I know that she wanted it (20 percent have been date raped).[2]

This is quite a different set of commandments to live by than that God gave to Moses on Mt. Sinai. Notice the contrasts:

> And God spoke all these words:
> "I am the Lord your God, who brought you out of Egypt, out of the land of slavery.
> "You shall have no other gods before me.
> "You shall not make for yourself an idol in the form of anything in heaven above or on the earth beneath or in the waters below. You shall not bow down to them or worship them; for I, the Lord your God, am a jealous God, punishing the children for the sin of the fathers to the third and fourth generation of those who hate me, but showing love to a thousand generations of those who love me and keep my commandments.
> "You shall not misuse the name of the Lord your God, for the Lord will not hold anyone guiltless who misuses his name.
> "Remember the Sabbath day by keeping it holy. Six days you shall labor and do all your work, but the seventh day is a Sabbath to the Lord your God. On it you shall not do any work, neither you, nor your son or daughter, nor your manservant or maidservant, nor your animals, nor the alien within your gates. For in six days the Lord made the heavens and the earth, the sea, and all that is in them,

but he rested on the seventh day. Therefore the Lord blessed the Sabbath day and made it holy.

"Honor your father and your mother, so that you may live long in the land the Lord your God is giving you.

"You shall not murder.

"You shall not commit adultery.

"You shall not steal.

"You shall not give false testimony against your neighbor.

"You shall not covet your neighbor's house. You shall not covet your neighbor's wife, or his manservant or maidservant, his ox or donkey, or anything that belongs to your neighbor."

Exodus 20:1–17

The differences between the Ten Commandments and the new commandments that Patterson and Kim have summarized are scary. Although Scripture makes clear statements about right and wrong, there is no clear definition of right and wrong in our culture today. Scripture declares that there is no God but God and that His day is holy. Our culture arrogantly says that God does not matter and asserts that our days are ours to use as we choose. The "shall nots" of Scripture have become the "I won't unless I want tos" of society's rules. The vacuum of moral belief is obvious.

Regardless of a person's religious beliefs, the Ten Commandments listed in Exodus provided the foundational values on which our society was built. Although there have always been corrupt individuals in every generation, society as a whole has functioned on the basis of these commandments—that it is wrong to steal, to lie, to murder, to commit adultery, and to want whatever belongs to one's neighbor. As recently as a generation or two ago, the Ten Commandments were still the fundamental guidelines by which American men lived. But, as we've seen, those guidelines have not been passed down to young men today. Our society has lost the foundation of biblical values that is necessary for its survival. Consequently, it is little wonder that these are shaky—even frightening—times for our culture, our families, and our government.

The new commandments summarized by Patterson and Kim provide ample evidence of the breakdown of community and family relationships. They reveal the inner struggles of adults from dysfunctional families. They also point to the great wound that has been created in the souls of children by the spiritual and emotional (and at times, physical) absence of fathers in their lives. Tragically, many other things have filled the void in the father-son relationship. The frantic, unchecked pursuit of something—anything—to fill the vacuum of deep masculine involvement has changed the moral code of our society.

Even these new commandments do not tell the whole story. Additional research by Patterson and Kim reveals even greater disintegration of fundamental values:

- 93 percent said that they and no one else determine what is and what is not moral.
- 84 percent confessed that they would violate the established rules of their religion.
- When asked what beliefs they would die for, 48 percent said, "none."
- Nearly half the population honestly feel that nobody knows them.
- 30 percent believe their mothers know them and 19 percent believe their fathers know them.
- 50 percent of eighteen- to twenty-four-year-olds honestly feel they received a good moral foundation from their parents.
- Lying has become a cultural trait in America, 91 percent of us lie regularly.
- Only 29 percent of Americans are virgins when they marry.

- 92 percent of sexually active people report having had ten or more lovers.
- Almost one-third of all married Americans (31 percent) have had or are having an affair.
- 62 percent of those having affairs believe there is nothing morally wrong with what they are doing.
- Among eighteen- to twenty-four-year olds, 61 percent revealed that they had lost their virginity by age sixteen; one in five kids report doing so by age thirteen.
- One in six adults across America were physically abused during childhood; one in seven adults were sexually abused (remember, most do not tell).
- One in four women will be sexually assaulted.
- As many as one in twenty Americans have participated in some ritual of Satanism or witchcraft.
- There is practically no sense of community anywhere in America today.
- 25 percent of Americans believe they will be divorced within the next five years.[3]

There is no denying that fundamental changes have occurred in the ethical and moral beliefs of people today. It is truly frightening that these changes happened so subtly that most of us were unaware of them until they produced the tragic circumstances we face today.

The breakup of the family is one factor that has led to the demise of traditional, fundamentally biblical values in American society. When nearly two out of three children no longer grow up in the same family in which they were born, children are terribly confused. When families break up and form new families, children have to deal with the dysfunction of four (and sometimes more) families of origin rather than just two. It is no wonder that children have trouble bonding with their parents and accepting their values.

The demise of the church as the center of community and social life has also contributed to the demise of biblical values in society. Today people no longer have to depend on the church for their social activities because so many other options exist. The church has also lagged behind in reaching out to meet the needs of people, so it appears irrelevant to much of society.

The tragic state of society today is, in part, a result of the lack of spiritual and emotional intimacy between fathers and their children, particularly their sons. This lack of emotional connection between father and son has a devastating impact on men in every stage of life, and on every level of society. How is it possible for one relationship to have such a powerful impact? The reason is that the father-son relationship is the most formative relationship in a man's life. The father-son relationship directs the development of the son's masculine identity and is the main avenue by which the guiding principles and values of life are passed from one generation to the next. When the father is not emotionally connected to his son, his son carries an inherent lack of trust in his father and his father's values, judgment, emotions, and spirituality.

I am not alone in my assessment. Storyteller and poet Robert Bly, researcher and motivational business speaker Stephen R. Covey, and pastor Gordon Dalbey have all written about the father-son wound and its impact on masculine identity and behavior. We will examine some of their findings and the helpful perspective they give us on the societal impact of the father-son wound.

A Loss of Intimacy and Emotional Bonding

Robert Bly has been a leader in creating an awareness of the issues men face today. He believes that the industrial revolution brought about a fundamental change in father-son relationships, a change in which much was lost. Prior to the industrial revolution, fathers and sons worked side by side in the fields. Even in the population centers, where men pursued non-agrarian occupations, sons often learned their trade or skills from their fathers. So fathers and sons had consistent contact. They worked together to enable the family to survive.

Something special happens when a son works side by side with his father. An emotional connection takes place that words cannot easily describe. As the father and son spend time together, a deep bonding occurs that provides a foundation for the boy's developing personality. Of course, if the father is shaming or abusive, the boy will be wounded at a deep level. But if the father is able to express his feelings and respond to his son's, the side-by-side contact with the father feeds the boy at a deep emotional level.

However, with the advent of automation, great factories were built and men moved from the fields to the assembly lines and offices. Sons no longer worked with their fathers. In fact, most sons no longer saw their fathers at work and often never even saw their workplace. Families no longer worked together in unity to survive. Men spent less time at home with their children. The mother became the emotional center of the family while the father became more of a peripheral part of family life.

Yet another aspect of the contemporary workplace has a great impact on the family and the level of father-son intimacy. The skills and methods of dealing with people and problems that make a man successful in his profession often do not work in the home. Consider the following examples:

At work, an engineer uses his ability to think factually and concretely. Computers, charts, and graphs are the mainstays of life. Because of these skills, many engineers are excellent financial planners who provide well for the future needs of their family. It can be difficult, however, for an engineer to respond to the feelings of his family members. At work he is used to responding to reasons and facts, but at home his family longs for him to respond to their feelings.

An attorney may be a great litigator. He may be a master with words, reasoning, and tactical strategies. He may be able, with one key question, to set up a desired response several questions later. But he may not know how to take off his judicial hat at home. So when family relationships are difficult and feelings are intense, his wife and children may feel as if they are dealing with a rigid, calculating judge rather than a husband and father.

A machinist may have to stand by the same machine all day long, dealing with precise tolerances to the hundredths or thousandths of inches. When he gets home, he may require a standard of perfection that no one in his family can hope to meet. He may have no tolerance for any deviation from pre-scribed activities and no ability to deal with feelings that are not easy to control.

The pastor whose duties run the gamut from spiritual leadership to administration to pastoral counseling to fundraising may come home and give spiritual advice for prob-lems that really need his personal, emotional response. Or he may be so burned out from dealing with people all day that he has no energy left to express the positive feelings he has for his family. Since he has already given his best all day long, his family gets what is left—his anger, frustration, and fatigue.

It takes quite a bit of wisdom and flexibility for a father to know when to lay down the weapons of the workplace and to follow his heart in dealing with his family. The weapons of the workplace help a father accomplish his goals and achieve success in the world. But if he is to have intimate family relationships, if he is to establish an emotional connection with his son, he must set those weapons aside and learn to under-stand and communicate through the language of the heart.

There is no substitute for an intimate, emotional connection between father and son. This connection cannot be made by a father who is physically or emotionally absent. It cannot be made by a father who functions at home in the same way he functions in the workplace. It takes time and emotional involvement for a father to establish intimacy with his son.

A New Ethic

The new commandments summarized earlier in this chapter clearly illustrate how much society's values have changed during the past few generations. Research done by Stephen R. Covey sheds light onto how and why this change has taken place. By studying what people had written about success in the past two hundred years, he discovered that there had been a change in the basic ethic of society during the past fifty years. Prior to World War II, a person's character was of utmost importance in achieving success. Since that time, however, a person's personality has become the key to success. Let us look further at the differences between a character ethic and a personality ethic.

Success literature written fifty to two hundred years ago emphasized a person's character, and the qualities Covey describes as "integrity, humility, fidelity, temperance, courage, justice, patience, industry, simplicity, modesty, and the Golden Rule."[4] Since then, however, writings about success have centered on "social image consciousness, techniques and quick fixes—with social band-aids and aspirin that addressed acute problems and sometimes even appeared to solve them temporarily but left the underlying chronic problems untouched to fester and resurface time and again."[5] In the new ethic, personality has become a more important ingredient of success than character. A person who has the right public image, behaviors, skills, and techniques will become successful. Outer appearance, the image of a person, is more important than who the person is on the inside.

This fundamental change has had a tremendous impact on both the family and father-son relationships. The personality ethic enables people to be "successful" without having any real substance inside. A person can maintain the outer trappings of success and be a total failure in virtually every significant relationship in life. A man can seem to make the impossible happen on the job, but not even be aware that he needs to respond to his son's emotional pain when his son is picked last for the soccer game at school. A man may have a successful, high-status position, but have no depth of core values to base his life upon or to pass on to his children.

When struggles occur (as they always will) in a relationship or family that functions according to a personality ethic, easy solutions take precedence over right solutions. For example, if one's sexual needs are not met in the marriage, it is much easier to have an affair than to search out and deal with the source of the problem. It is much easier to abandon a relationship than to resolve recurring difficulties. Fidelity or a lifelong commitment to one person, both highly valued traits of the old character ethic, are now passé.

The new personality ethic yields tragic results in father-son relationships. When the personality ethic is dominant, the strong character values that have traditionally been passed down from father to son are lost. A son may notice that his father does whatever is necessary to be successful in business, whether his actions are ethical or not. He may see that his father has just the right haircut, wears just the right suits, and drives just the right car; but he may also notice that his father has little initiative to do things that interest his son. A son may hear his father talk about a commitment to God, but see that his father is a little too friendly with the neighbor's wife. He may hear his father talk about how he cheats on his taxes. When the father lives according to the personality ethic, he has little strength of character to pass on to his son.

The lack of commitment fostered by the personality ethic also contributes to the break up and abandonment of families by fathers. Sons get even less time with their fathers. Today, 50 percent of all fathering is done on an every-other-weekend basis. Children can no longer count on both parents being a part of their lives while they are growing up. Please understand that I have no desire to single out or shame fathers who find themselves in this situation. I am only trying to create an awareness of the impact of broken father-son relationships so that fathers can take steps to curb this destructive trend and do whatever is necessary to build emotionally intimate relationships with their sons.

The Television Image of Tough Masculinity

Changes in society over the past five decades have diminished the emotional bridge between the grandfather, father, and son to such an extent that, for the first time, a segment of people has emerged whose moral code has been primarily developed by television. Saturday morning cartoons, MTV, *Rambo,* evening sitcoms, Hulk Hogan, *The Terminator,* and a variety of sports heroes often fill the void God intended the father to fill in a boy's life. The characters the boy sees on television have become his models; they shape his identity and dictate his values.

You may be tempted to think that I am exaggerating the influence television has on a boy's development, but I am not. I regularly counsel men who did not have deep and meaningful relationships with their fathers and in the absence of those relationships adopted the values and images of masculinity that they saw on television. One young sex addict in his early thirties truly could not imagine living faithfully with only one woman during his lifetime. His main idea of love and romance had come from "Loveboat." It took months of therapy before he began to realize that not everyone has sex before marriage. This was a totally new concept for him to consider.

Warren Farrell, author of *The Liberated Man*, has written about the standard of masculinity our television-oriented culture communicates. Farrell refers to John Wayne as the "Moses of Masculinity" and portrays him with a tablet that lists the "ten commandments" of traditional maledom:

1. Thou shalt not cry or expose other feelings of emotion, fear, weakness, sympathy, empathy or involvement before thy neighbor.
2. Thou shalt not be vulnerable, but honor and respect the "logical," "practical," or "intellectual"—as thou definest them.
3. Thou shalt not listen except to find fault.
4. Thou shalt condescend to women in the smallest and biggest of ways.
5. Thou shalt control thy wife's body.
6. Thou shalt have no other egos before thee.
7. Thou shalt have no other breadwinners before thee.
8. Thou shalt not be responsible for housework—before anybody.
9. Thou shalt honor and obey the straight and narrow pathway to success: job specialization.
10. Thou shalt have an answer to all problems at all times. [6]

These commandments summarize well the standards of the "tough man." He faces the most challenging issues with no hint of fear. He bears even the greatest pain without flinching. Like John Wayne, the tough man only shows pain when he is shot—then he grits his teeth and defeats the bad guy anyway.

But the impact of these rules is staggering:

Men live, on the average, almost 10 years less than women;
Males commit suicide 300 percent more often;
All the major diseases leading toward death show significantly higher rates for males;
Men have higher murder and assault and battery rates; and
Men show a significantly higher rate of drug and alcohol abuse. [7]

There can be no doubt that the masculine values and images portrayed on television are detrimental to men. There is also no doubt that young boys soak up these values. The tragedy, however, is not that television images are of such poor quality. The tragedy is that when fathers do not bond with their sons, their sons fill that void with whatever they can find.

Boys will always find heroes. When those heroes are cartoon or movie characters, boys soak up the values, attitudes, and fantasies projected on the television or movie screen. If the boy's hero is his coach, he will soak up the "tough man" values and attitudes that the coach projects. When a father is not emotionally connected with his son, these are the models that will influence his son's sexual identity, his definition of right and wrong, his idea of what life is about, and his concept of how relationships work.

The Untapped Strength of Men

Despite the devastating changes in our young men and our society that I have highlighted in this chapter, I believe in the untapped strength of men and the powerful, positive roles they can play in both family and society. I am particularly excited about the significant source of spiritual, emotional, and relational strength the Christian community of men can provide. However, Christian men are presently a greatly underdeveloped resource. Most Christian men are unaware of their deep father-son wound, so they remain its victims. That deep, unhealed hurt holds every aspect of a man's life hostage—his career, his family life, and his spiritual life. I am convinced that the way for men to realize their potential and fulfill their God-given responsibilities—to themselves, their families, the church, and society—lies in recognizing the impact of the father-son wound and taking steps toward healing.

CHAPTER 4

The Impact of the Father Wound on a Man's Family Life

When a man reaches his twenties, he sets out to make his place in the world. It is an exciting time for him as many aspects of his life begin to change. He starts to put most of his life's energy into building his career and, if he is married, into his marriage. He may become acutely aware of the burden he carries to meet his family's financial needs and may work fifty to seventy hours a week in order to provide the best of everything for the family he loves. He may jump through hoop after hoop in an effort to meet his driving need for achievement and his family's need for financial security.

In the midst of these compelling concerns, a man has little time for friends. There is no time to maintain close, caring friendships with his peers, or to develop relationships with older men who could support him in his growth as a husband and father and guide him as he navigates the twists and turns of his career. At this point in life, a young man's energies are focused on priorities other than relationships.

Unfortunately, this is also a dangerous time for a young man. Every man needs close relationships with other men. When those relationships are lacking in a young man's life, trouble lies ahead. The emptiness a man feels inside from the woundedness of his relationship with his father can only be filled through relationships with other men and with God. Often, however, a man will seek to fill that masculine woundedness through relationships with women, but women cannot meet this deep emotional need. A man who shares his deeper feelings exclusively with women is either in trouble emotionally or is setting himself up for trouble later on. When a man seeks to have his deep, emotional needs fulfilled through relationships with women, he, his marriage, and his family will suffer.

This period of life is also risky because at this age most men have not become aware of their father-son wound, so they are disconnected from their feelings. When a man is out of touch with his feelings of grief, emptiness, and loss, he is simply unable to recognize the emotional needs of others around him. He cannot really identify with another person's feelings or what they are going through unless he has some understanding and connection with his own deep feelings. Since family relationships are emotionally intimate, an emotionally disconnected man will have a destructive impact on his loved ones.

When a Man Focuses on Relationships with Women

When a man tries to soothe his deep wound through relationships with women rather than through healing relationships with men, his marriage *will* suffer. There is no way a man's marriage can possibly escape the destructive consequences of his dependence on emotionally fulfilling relationships with women other than his wife. His children, although perhaps to a lesser degree, will also suffer.

He may seek emotional bonds with women. Many men learn early on that they cannot share their hurts, fears, or worries with their fathers. When they become adults, these men do not even consider other men as a possible source of comfort or support. When they feel pain or face trouble, they do not for a minute think of seeking out other men. Since it is uncomfortable and often depressing to face the deep grief they feel inside and grapple with the emotional loss they have suffered in their relationships with their fathers, many men turn to women to meet that need. They find it much more comfortable to be understood and cared for by women than to take the risk of developing close relationships with men.

A man may even marry a woman because he feels that she really understands and cares about him, and can fill the deep emotional void he feels within. But such a relationship carries tremendous risk. The truth is, no woman can ever fill the need a man has for deep, emotionally connected relationships with other men. When a man marries a woman because he feels understood and cared for by her, he has placed tremendously unrealistic—in fact, impossible—expectations on her. Later in life, when the man realizes that his wife has not filled those unrealistic expectations, he may find another woman who seems to understand him better or care for him more deeply. He may go through life discovering woman after woman, expecting each one to meet a need that no woman can ever meet.

When a man's deep emotional needs are not met through healing relationships with other men, he will often have poor boundaries with women. He may find it easier to talk with women than to talk with men. So when he has difficulty talking with his wife, it may be easier for him to share his frustrations and problems with a woman coworker or friend. The problem is, when a man develops a sharing relationship with a woman, he is bonding with her. Establishing an emotional bond with another woman is a violation of his marital boundaries. When this happens, his wife will often feel a loss or distancing in her relationship with her husband, which of course damages the marriage.

Furthermore, the emotional bonding with another woman often sets the foundation for an extramarital affair. When a man has an affair, his marriage not only suffers, his children suffer as well. A man who is having an affair pours his time and emotional energy into the new relationship, not into his relationship with his children. So his children suffer feelings of abandonment and emotional distancing from their father, even if they do not know he is having an affair.

His views of sexuality will be distorted. Men who seek healing relationships with women may have a distorted sexual image of women. They may also have a tendency to move toward sex-love addiction, seeking romance and sex as a way to fill the deep wound they feel inside. Both of these characteristics destroy a marital relationship.

When a man has an unrealistic expectation of what a sexual relationship with a woman should be, he may be driven to find the "perfect woman" to match his fantasy. This fantasy often has its source in the way women are portrayed on television, in the movies, and in pornographic material. In reality he is looking for a sexual goddess who is always sexually interested, sexually assertive, and sexually responsive.

No woman on earth matches this fantasy; yet the fantasy persists, and it is highly injurious to real-life marriages. A man who lives under the illusion of this fantasy cannot be truly empathetic with his wife. He cannot comprehend the possibility that his wife may not always be interested in sex. He does not understand that his wife's sexual desire can be affected by spiritual, emotional, or physical factors. When the reality of his relationship with a real, human wife shatters his sexual fantasy, he will become angry. This anger further damages their relationship and leads to greater emotional distance between them.

If a man tends toward sex-love addiction, he often has only superficial or sexually-oriented relationships with women. If the primary bond in his relationship with his wife is sexual, the marriage will not last. The truth is, this type of man relates primarily to sexual excitement, not to the person with whom he has a sexual relationship. As time progresses, a woman who is the object of a sex-love addiction will feel used, abused, and manipulated. This kind of interaction is destructive to any intimate relationship between a man and a woman, particularly the marriage relationship.

When a man is obsessed with sexual fantasies, a fundamental disrespect for women results. This lack of respect may be evident in the sexual comments he makes about or to women and the dirty jokes he tells. The man may also fantasize about the women he meets or sees, visually undressing them just by looking at them. Women notice these behaviors. They feel violated and unsafe, and will usually distance themselves from these men.

When a man indulges in these fantasies, he is betraying his wife. Inwardly, he is always looking for greener pastures, hoping to find the more perfect woman. Although many men believe that their fantasies do not harm anyone, there is a fine line between recreational fantasy, obsession, and making the fantasy a reality.

One way men make their fantasies seem more real is by compulsive masturbation, which becomes a means of relaxation and self-nurturing. Rather than seeking relationships with other men who can support him as he works out difficult issues in life, a man may use sexually explicit television programs, magazines, and videos as stimuli to perpetuate his fantasies. These actions may make him feel better for a time, but they destroy the emotional bridge between a man and his wife and represent the breakdown of the man's spiritual relationship with God as well.

There is hope in healing. Doug is one man who depended on relationships with women to meet his emotional needs. Although he loved his wife and children, he had no boundaries in his relationships with women. It was easy for him to share his problems and frustrations with women at work. Many times a woman at work would become his primary source of emotional support and then a sexual partner. His problem was made worse by his frequent business trips for his company. In each city he regularly visited, he had at least one woman, if not two, whom he would call and go out with to talk. Usually the two of them would spend the night together.

Life began to change for Doug when his wife found out about one of his many affairs. She gave him a choice: either they begin counseling or their marriage would be over. Doug agreed and their counselor soon recommended that he begin individual therapy as well. That is when Doug came to me.

As I worked with Doug, it became apparent that he was sexually addicted. He could not even remember the number of women with whom he had sex. He was so involved with his addiction that he had not even considered the possibility of contracting AIDS. Although he considered himself to be a Christian, he felt no guilt about betraying his wife or disobeying God. He was living two completely separate lives. He believed that his sexual behavior harmed no one, and therefore did not matter.

Whenever I counsel a man such as Doug who has a sex-love addiction, I suggest that he attend a twelve-step group for that addiction. I also encourage him to form his own support group of men who are committed to being emotionally vulnerable and spiritually supportive of one another. And I strongly urge him to make a connection with his inner child so that he can become increasingly aware of his feelings.

Doug laughed at my suggestions. He did not believe it was possible for men to be supportive or understanding. In his mind women, not men, offered understanding, sympathy, and nurturing. He saw other men only as rivals he competed against in the workplace. Doug also thought the idea of connecting with his inner child was silly. He went along with my suggestions, however, because his marriage depended on his continued counseling.

During our sessions, I began to explore Doug's childhood. Doug had been raised primarily by his mother and had few memories of his relationship with his father. As an adult, Doug had generally felt angry when he was around his father, so he had kept his distance. To get to the root of these memories, I asked Doug to close his eyes and picture himself as a young boy. An image of himself at seven years old came into his mind. I asked him what that little boy was feeling.

With surprise in his voice, Doug said, "He feels pain on the back of his legs and lower back."

"What is happening to the little boy?" I asked.

Doug's body began to shake and he began to cry. "His father is hitting him with a belt and yelling and screaming at him. His father is telling him that he is a bad, bad boy and that he will never be anything good."

"What would you like to do to help that boy?" I asked.

"I want to tell his father he has no right to hit his son like that. I want to tell him to get out of the room and stay out!"

"Let me know when you have done that for that hurt little boy." When Doug nodded his head, I continued, "Now take that little boy to a safe place where his father cannot hurt him."

Doug took his seven-year-old little boy to a safe place surrounded by boulders next to a mountain stream. I then asked, "How do you want to comfort that little boy?"

"I don't know if I can," Doug answered. "The little boy is afraid of men."

"Tell the little boy you understand," I suggested. "His father, the most significant man in his life, has hurt him badly. Tell the little boy that you and I understand why he doesn't trust men. Tell him that we feel sadness for him because he has suffered so much hurt."

Doug began sobbing once more. "He wants me to hold him, but I have to be careful because his back and legs are bruised."

I encouraged Doug to picture a warm, beautiful beam of sunlight coming down from his Heavenly Father. I told him that the light could touch and heal the places where the little boy was wounded and that it could melt away the bad things his father had said about him. I told him it was okay to hurt and to cry. I told him that God had made him in a special way and that he could learn to become the man God intended him to be. Doug continued to cry and comfort that child as he envisioned this healing for the child within.

The process of connecting with his inner child and healing from the deep wounds he suffered at his father's hand opened up Doug's memories and helped him understand his resistance to seeking supportive relationships with other men. He realized that his father had given him a strong message: men cannot be trusted. He recognized that his mother had been his only safe parent, but that their relationship was emotionally incestuous because she continually shared with him her frustration and anger related to his father. Doug remembered that in early adolescence he had learned how good it felt to be held by a girl. He also recalled the times that his father had talked with him about the affairs he was having. And he remembered being sexually molested by a neighbor who paid him to perform oral sex.

These memories helped melt away his resistance to actively working a twelve-step program. Through his twelve-step work, he was able to feel the healthy guilt and shame of betraying his wife and disobeying God. He began to feel in his heart what he had known intellectually as a Christian. He began to heal.

Now, Doug's primary relationships are with men, and his boundaries with women are firm. He is alone with a woman only to conduct business. If he begins to desire her sexually, he contacts a supportive male friend to help him work through the crisis. If he is away from home overnight, he finds an Overcomers Outreach or other twelve-step meeting to attend. Doug still has much work to do in rebuilding the emotional bridges to his wife and children, but by connecting with his inner child and by developing relationships with men, he has found a way of healing.

When a Man Can't Feel

Clearly the wife and children of a man who is isolated from healing, supportive relationships with other men feel the impact of his pain when he seeks to fill his emptiness through relationships with other women. But this is not the only way a man who is wounded in his relationship with his father carries his pain into his family life. One of the easiest ways for a man (and a woman too) to deal with inner pain is to distance or disconnect himself from that pain. The problem with this solution is that he also disconnects himself from all other feelings. When a man has not come to grips with his inner feelings, he may be unable to feel anything. If he is incapable of feeling emotion or understanding the emotions of others, family intimacy is destroyed.

From a very early age, boys are taught to suppress their feelings. They learn early on that "big boys don't cry," no matter what. So they learn to deny whatever physical, emotional, or spiritual pain they feel. They learn that "real men" can conquer anything and do not need to depend on help from others. They learn to feel no pain or fear and to show no weakness. This creates great trouble for men and their families.

Men who don't feel emotionally, don't feel physically. The impact of the "feel no pain, show no weakness" mentality is obvious at lunch time on Sundays. In almost every restaurant groups of older women—widows—eat together, enjoying the benefit of their dead husbands' hard work. Why is there an abundance of widows? Because in America today, men usually live ten years less than women. Why do men die earlier? One reason is due to their denial of feelings.

The denial of emotional pain and denial of physical pain go hand in hand; a man who is disconnected from what he feels emotionally tends to be disconnected from what he feels physically. As a result, men often ignore their aches and pains until they have major problems. Illnesses that could have been treated easily are ignored until they require major intervention. The first time many men seek regular medical care is after they have a major heart attack. What a sad result of not being in touch with one's feelings!

A shortened life span and its impact on the family is not the only painful result of a husband and father who is disconnected from his feelings. A man who is basically unaware of his feelings often has difficulty communicating with his wife and children. He finds it difficult to work through problems, respect his wife, and be sensitive to the emotional needs of those around him. He also tends to be very shaming to his wife and children.

Men who are disconnected emotionally have trouble relating to their families. When a man is disconnected from his own feeling life, he is out of touch not only with his own feelings but with the feelings of his family. Unless he has made some connection with his own hurt in his relationship with his father, he is incapable of feeling what others feel or feeling the emotional impact of his behavior on others.

For example, a father may be very angry but may not recognize that he feels that way. His wife and children will certainly know he is angry! However, if they try to tell him so, he will reject their perceptions of his anger. He may well respond, "No I'm not! I'll show you what *real* anger is!" To him, nothing short of absolute rage qualifies as anger.

What is happening in a situation like this is that the father is unable to accept the reality of his family's perception. His perceptions are the only reality he will accept. It is a big growth step for a man to accept his family's perception of him as real regardless of how he feels about it, and to respond to their feelings. It is vitally important for a man to take a hard look at himself and respond to his family's feelings about him because, if they perceive him as being angry, they probably feel a little afraid of him. This fear damages their relationship with him.

Unfortunately, most men have not dealt enough with their own grief in relationship to their father-son wound to begin to understand, respect, or respond empathetically to another person's feelings. They do not have a clue as to what their families are trying to tell them. They are so filled with their own shame and denial of feelings that their only response is defensiveness and even more anger.

I worked with a family in which Andy, the husband and father, truly could not believe that he was a controlling, angry man. He was in such intense denial that he genuinely believed that his problems originated solely in his wife and children; yet anyone who was close to him knew he was angry. In addition to this, he carried a tremendous load of shame and could not allow himself to acknowledge the truth about himself. This is not unusual. Men who have high levels of shame find it difficult to admit their wrongs, because then they believe they are really bad. When men have some recovery going, however, they can acknowledge their failure, reflect on it, apologize to those they have wronged, and go on. Andy, however, stayed in denial, with tragic results. Eventually his wife left him to secure the emotional safety of their children.

The need to always be in control of one's family, and the anger that results when a man cannot be, is a big issue for many men. A man needs relationships with other men in order to identify and work through some of those feelings. Tom Watson, Jr., a father of six children, shares some of what it was like for him to deal with feelings related to his work at IBM and his family:

> By the time I got home, there would be nothing left of me. I'd walk in and find the usual disorder of a large household—one of the kids had shot a BB gun at a passing car, or two of them were fighting, or somebody had bad grades. These things would strike me as crises that needed to be resolved right away, and yet I had no energy to bring to bear. I'd feel a desperate wish for somebody

else to step in and make the decisions so I didn't have to. That's when I'd blow up. The kids would scatter like quail and Olive would catch the brunt of my frustration. . . . It took me years to grasp the fundamental difference between running a company and heading a family. IBM was like driving a car: when I came to a corner, I could steer around it very nicely, and off the car would go down a new road. I hit bumps here and there, but generally the car went where I wanted. With my family, this wasn't the case. The family was more like a car with two steering wheels, or multiple steering wheels, and only one of them belonged to me. I kept trying to exercise more control than I had.

When I saw I could not bend my wife and children to my will, I'd feel totally thwarted and boxed in. Those were the blackest moments of my adult life. An argument with Olive and the kids would sometimes make me so morose that the only thing I could do was hole up. I'd lock myself in my dressing room and Olive would stand on the other side of the door and try to get me to come out. Finally she'd reach the end of her rope. She'd call my brother and say, "Can't you come cheer Tom up?" Dick would come down from New Canaan. He always knew how to make my responsibilities seem lighter and draw me back into the world.[1]

How fortunate Tom Watson, Jr. was to have a man in his life who could help him deal with his feelings and bring him back to reality.

Men who are disconnected from their feelings will, without even trying to do so, shame their children. Children have a deep emotional need to be listened to and understood. When a father does not respond to his child's feelings, when he says or acts as if what the child is feeling or saying is unimportant, the child feels shamed. Shame creates tremendous emotional damage. It makes children feel as if something about them is bad.

Remember, children need an emotional bond with their fathers. They need understanding and empathy. It is impossible for a father to truly identify with what his children are going through unless he understands some of his own feelings. I can see this in my own life. I have four children, two teenagers and two preschoolers. I have developed a deeper emotional connection with the younger children than I had with the older children when they were young. I was not in touch with my anger, shame, and fear when my older children were young, so I could not be as responsive as I can be now.

Let me share an example of this newfound empathy. One of the younger children had a massive temper tantrum in Taco Bell not long ago. I tried everything I could think of to get her to quiet down (yes, even therapists do not always know how to deal with their children) and finally had to take her out to the car and give her one swat on the bottom. The spanking was more symbolic than actual. It caused no physical pain, but it had a tremendous impact on my daughter. In fact, two days later she timidly approached me in the family room and said, "Daddy, somebody spilled Coke all over the entryway."

I had seen her bike and the can of Coke there earlier, so I suspected what had happened. But I also saw the fear in her eyes and the tension in her body. "Are you afraid you're going to get a spanking?" I asked. She started to cry. I sat down, held her, and said, "I'm sorry. There is a big difference between what happened at Taco Bell and this accident. We'll clean this up. It's no big deal." When I said that, she relaxed and the tears went away. I also learned and felt how devastating corporal punishment is . . . and I wonder now if it is even an option.

I missed a lot of that kind of interaction when my older children were young, but it is never too late. Now when I overreact or become angry with them, I can see the hurt in their eyes and know that I need to reach out to them, to respond differently. I have the chance to repair some of the damage that occurred in our day-to-day lives together, damage that I was not even aware of before.

Men who are disconnected from their feelings often are unable to respect or care for their wives. The extent to which a man is connected to his feelings dramatically affects his marriage. The more a man feels emotionally, the more he can identify with and honor his wife's needs. The more a man is divorced from his feelings, the less he is able to identify or care about his wife's desires. If a man is not in touch with his emotions, he will not even notice how his wife feels. This is true of his wife's sexual needs as well as her emotional needs. His wife may tell her husband she has had a hard day, for example, and may receive only a passing grunt in response. No wife feels respected in that kind of interaction.

This lack of respect is also evident in a man's response to his wife's hopes and aspirations. A man who is not connected to his feelings is often fearful of and unable to support his wife's personal development. If his wife reaches a point in life where she wants to pursue something important to her, such as going to college to earn a degree, going to work, assuming a particular responsibility at church, or even having children, he may not have room for that in his life. He may not want to make the necessary adjustment so his wife can pursue those interests. He may sabotage her efforts, even if those activities would obviously benefit her.

I'd like to retell an old story that Robert Bly relates about a man who lacked both deep respect and the ability to truly care for the woman he loved.

A long, long time ago, a young man would stand by his window at night, looking out at the starry sky. He would say to the stars, "I wish, I wish, that a beautiful woman would come to me, take care of me, and love me completely and deeply." This was his nightly ritual. Not a night went by that he did not make this wish to the stars.

One night, one of the stars that glowed so brightly came down into his room and became a beautiful woman. The young man looked at her, he desired her, and they made love all night long. When morning came, he looked at the woman and said, "What am I to do with you?"

"I don't know," she answered.

"I can't leave you alone here," the young man said. "Someone might find you."

So he took a bottle with a stopper and asked the beautiful woman to go inside, which she did. He put the stopper in the bottle, tucked it into his pocket, and went about his business. That night when he came home, he opened the bottle to let the woman out, and they made love again all night long. In the morning, he returned her to her place in the bottle. He repeated this ritual for many, many days. Although he barely noticed, the woman's eyes became redder and redder with each passing day.

One morning, when the man let her out of the bottle, she said, "That is enough!" She then reached into her pocket, pulled out three seeds, and threw them down to the ground.

Immediately a giant tree shot up to the heavens. The woman began climbing up the tree, toward the starry heavens.

"Don't go!" the young man called after her. "Please don't leave me. I can't live without you."

She ignored his pleas and continued climbing upward, so he followed her.

"Don't follow me," she warned. "You cannot come with me. It will be the death of you."

The young man ignored her words and continued to follow her, pleading and begging her to stay. But then he looked down and saw the ground far below him. Suddenly he fell and died.[2]

Women are no different from men in their need for personal growth. The man in the story only valued her sexually, not her person, not *her* dreams, goals, and desires. If they have a growing desire or call to do something, they need to do it. A man who is not in touch with his feelings does not realize that this is true about his wife. He does not understand that if a woman cannot pursue her God-given desires and leading, her whole body and spirit will suffer. Her suffering can lead to depression, illness, and even death. He does not realize that if he ignores his wife's feelings and needs, their relationship will not last.

When a man is emotionally connected, however, he will feel the value of his wife's personal development and will fully support her, even if it means making personal sacrifices. I, for example, love to play basketball. If I could, I would still spend many evenings at the gym, playing in some kind of league (which I did for a number of years). But music is important to my wife Karen. She comes alive and feels a great sense of purpose and fulfillment when she is involved in church music. So every Wednesday night the kids are my responsibility from 4:00 P.M. on, and on Sunday mornings it is my responsibility to get them ready for church. My commitment to the family at these times is necessary so that Karen can participate in choir and handbell activities. It is important that she knows I'll be there to take care of the family so she can pursue her interests.

I still play basketball and work out at a health club several times a week, so my needs are not ignored. I make sure, however, that I do not do those things at times when they prevent Karen's needs from being met. This is one way I am able to show her how deeply I care for her. I would not be able to do this if I were not in touch with my own feelings.

Men who aren't well connected with their feelings also lack a basic respect for women and children in general. They have a decreased sensitivity to the impact of their words and actions upon others. Many men today who are age fifty and older have for years made lewd comments to women they work with and told off-color jokes. Such behavior is now considered to be sexual harassment (and actually has always been harassment). Many of these men are now in shock because they considered their actions to be perfectly normal and never realized they were doing anything offensive.

Regrettably, the Christian culture is not exempt from this lack of respect and care for women and children. Some traditional Christian values and beliefs, which are not truly biblical but have been generally accepted as Christian, have failed to recognize the value of women and to respect their role in church and family life. Some churches, for example, have placed so much emphasis on the wife's submission to her husband in all circumstances (even if the husband is abusive) that it has fostered codependency among women and enabled some husbands to remain in their addictions.

Current attitudes toward abortion are further evidence of men's lack of emotional connection, their inability to feel the impact of their actions. In our society, abortion is viewed as an exclusively feminine issue. It is of course a feminine issue, but its a masculine one as well. Men participate in creating every new life, yet many have so little care for that life. The fact that men in our society care so little about their unborn children reveals a great deal about men. There is something very sad about a father who is so out of touch with himself or so selfish that he does not value the new life he has created. When a man becomes aware of his father-son wound and begins to really feel what is inside, he changes. He becomes aware of the impact of his words, because he can empathize and imagine the impact upon himself if the same words were spoken to him. He is able to respect and care for his wife in ways he could not even imagine before. He is able to listen to the needs of his children and respond to them out of the fullness of his heart. Men who are emotionally connected are also spiritually activated and will take steps to meet the needs they see and feel in church and family. Men who are in touch with their feelings have within them a deep and powerful concern for the new life they create and will be strong advocates for that new life, doing everything they can to enable it to develop into adulthood. By healing from their own woundedness, men are able to help heal the wounds of others.

CHAPTER 5

The Impact of the Father Wound on a Man's Career

Whether or not he is able to recognize it, a son instinctively feels a sense of loss when he has no emotional connection with his father. He feels this loss in their relationship, but he also feels the loss in his masculine identity. The emotional bridge between father and son touches the heart of the son's masculine soul: his identity not only as a son, but as a man. So it should be no surprise that as a boy grows into manhood, he devotes much of his energy toward trying to build an emotional bridge to his father.

Since a man's work is an important part of his life (and is often viewed by our culture as *the* most important part) it should be no surprise that a man's career is often the stage upon which he tries to build that emotional bridge to his father. Natural ability, training, and opportunity certainly play key roles in a man's career, but for most men the father wound is the dominant force. A man may become addicted to work, allow his work to replace his family relationships, be easily manipulated by his employers, be driven to achieve the impossible, have trouble getting or keeping a job, or may feel unworthy and work himself into an early grave—all in an effort to prove his worth to his dad. These possibilities, and many more, relate directly to a man's relationship with his father.

Seeking Approval Through Achievement

A son may try to reach his father through achievement. As we saw earlier, Tom Watson, Jr. is a prime example of a son who hungered for an emotional bond with his father. Like many sons, he tried to earn his father's recognition and acceptance through remarkable achievements. He guided IBM, the company his father founded, as it grew into a mammoth, worldwide corporation. In the late 1940s, just a few years after he took over management of the firm, he doubled the company's gross sales—from $70 million to $140 million. All the time, he longed for his father to notice his accomplishments. He hungered for a clear and direct acknowledgment of his success and an affirmation that his father accepted him as both a man and a businessman.

That affirmation did not come easily. The elder Watson trusted his son in some areas of the business, but considered him to be totally incompetent in others—and was not afraid to tell him so. Finally, after one heated discussion, the younger Watson received a note from his father that said:

100%
Confidence
Appreciation
Admiration
Love
Dad[1]

Not too long after that, his father formally passed the leadership of IBM to his son.

For many men, the drive to achieve in order to gain their fathers' approval begins at an early age. Young boys often seek to earn their fathers' approval through achievement in the same sports in which their fathers participated. You can see this struggle for acceptance at almost any youth league baseball, basketball, soccer, or football game in the country. If you look carefully, you can spot the boy on the team who keeps scanning the crowd to see if his father will show up. You can almost feel his loss when his father is not there, perhaps because work, alcohol, or a woman other than the boy's mother occupies his father's attention. You can see the despair in the eyes of the boy who sits on the bench, a boy who works so hard yet does not have the skills to be out on the field where he can hear his father cheer for him. You can see bitter disappointment in the eyes of the son who yearns for the cheers, compliments, and smiles his father directs toward his teammates but not toward him because he is not the best.

There was a boy like this on my son's soccer team. The boy was a joy to watch. He was a natural sprinter who ran effortlessly and could control the ball too. He moved across the field like lightning. The other team knew that if he got the ball, it would be a one-on-one challenge between him and the goalie—and that the goalie usually lost.

During one game, my son's team was winning and everyone had played well. Once again his star teammate broke through and headed toward the goal. This time, however, things went differently. Another teammate was close by and, instead of scoring, the boy passed the ball to him so his teammate could have the joy of the goal. It was a beautiful example of teamwork and sharing; yet when the young speedster made it to the sidelines, his father was furious because he had not made the score himself. Throughout the season, that boy's father never enjoyed his son's accomplishments. The boy kept running and working as hard as he could, but he never received the acceptance and affirmation he so deeply desired. His father never put his arm around him and said, "Great job, son. I'm proud of you."

When a boy reaches adulthood, this intense desire to prove himself to his father does not just go away. Although he may not realize its source, it provides the inward motivation that keeps driving him to succeed. The young man often looks to his bosses and supervisors for the approval he intensely desires from his father. This desire is so intense that the son may not be aware of what he is doing until he faces some kind of emotional, spiritual, or physical crisis.

A young man's drive for achievement may have a variety of results. Some men have such a powerful desire to succeed that their career becomes more important than their families. A man may be so intent on climbing the corporate ladder that he accepts any transfers his company requests, no matter how great the impact upon his family. Another man may be so intent on gaining approval that he will agree to attend an unscheduled meeting rather than decline so he can attend his son's birthday party. For many men, the desire for fatherly approval results in work addiction.

Work Addiction

When a man yearns for his father's approval, he easily falls into the trap of overwork. Overwork often brings approval from a man's employer and perhaps the appearance of respect from a man's coworkers. Success at work makes a man feel important. It makes him feel good enough to ignore some of the pain he feels inside. These good feelings set a man up to devote increasing amounts of time and energy to his work.

But those good feelings are based on performance only. Once a man gets away from the workplace, he loses them. Work then becomes a type of emotional "fix." That is why some men become depressed and even die within a few years of retirement. They based their sense of self-worth on their success in the workplace and when their basis for self-worth was removed, they had no reason to continue living.

Work addiction also has physiological side effects. Once a man becomes involved in overwork and compulsive activity, he consistently experiences a level of excitement and intensity that is difficult to achieve otherwise. When that occurs, he can easily become addicted to the resulting adrenaline high. Even a major crisis provides an exciting diversion for him. If he stops working at his normal level of intensity, he will feel fatigued and depressed. These are the same feelings a person who withdraws from alcohol or drugs experiences.

Men who succumb to the psychological and physiological effects of work addiction have room for little else in their lives. They can work incredibly long hours and hardly notice that they spend most of their lives away from their families. To a work-addicted man, a forty-hour week feels like a part-time job—even a sixty-hour week seems short. Any friendships a work-addicted man may have are usually superficial, work-centered relationships. The work-addicted man is mentally and emotionally obsessed with the next task on his list. He has little, if any, awareness of who he is or how he feels deep inside and may be nearly oblivious to what is happening around him.

Tom, a client of mine, is a classic example of work addiction in action. One day, while driving down a busy street, he was talking to one of his crews via his car phone and to the men in his warehouse via his shortwave radio. As he was madly scratching down a few notes on a pad of paper—surprise—he hit the back of the car in front of him! The driver of the other car came back to talk with him but could not get his attention until Tom had finished his phone call. Tom then called for a tow truck and asked the man at the towing company to have a rental car waiting for him at the body shop. While he was in the tow truck, Tom continued making phone calls and using the shortwave radio in the truck. As soon as his car arrived at the body shop, he jumped into the waiting rental car and drove off!

The accident had caused thousands of dollars of damage to his car, yet it inconvenienced Tom for less than an hour. He didn't miss a beat in keeping his company going. Can you imagine the adrenaline overload and added stress his body endured? Only a work addict can operate this way. The addiction takes a tremendous toll on his life and family and, for some men, even replaces their family relationships.

Replacing Family Relationships with Work

To a certain extent, the familial nature of some work relationships can be positive, such as when a young man has the privilege of finding a mentor—an older man who serves as a guide and supporter for the younger man as he develops in his profession. Samuel Osherson, who has extensively studied how a man's life is shaped by his relationship with his father, says, "A powerful mentor may speak to the hunger vulnerable young men have for a strong, all-accepting father-hero, whom we can love and revere unambivalently. . . . For many young men, mentors truly become the better fathers they yearn for."[2]

The mentor (or at times supervisors, company managers, or peers) provides camaraderie, affirmation, and value for the younger man. These elements are vital for a man's continued development, and are often the very things missing from the man's relationship with his father. Yet even this good relationship has a toxic side.

Consider Jim, who was assigned a mentor when he first joined a major computer company. The older man had been with the company for years and was highly skilled in his particular area. His job was to educate Jim about the company, its policies, and how to work successfully within the organization. As Jim worked beside this man, a warm, supportive relationship developed. Jim felt comfortable enough to begin to share some of his personal struggles with him. He talked about how difficult it was to move his family to a new area and his fear that he would not succeed. His mentor assured Jim of his continued support during this period of adjustment. He recognized Jim's skills and encouraged him to continue developing his potential.

Jim was deeply touched by his relationship with this man. At last the needs of the little boy within him, needs that had been untouched by his own father, were being met. Hungry for this nourishment, Jim became like a little boy who was trying to please his dad. He began to overwork. He was eager to go to work and do something more to please this older man who had become like a father to him. It became harder and harder for him to leave work and go home to his family because his deepest emotional needs were being met on the job.

Jim's situation is not all that unique. When a man's emotional needs are met through work, it is easy for work and work relationships to take the place of his family relationships. On the job, the people around him think he is a great guy because he is doing wonderful things and producing so much. He may receive more affirmation from his secretary than he ever receives from his wife. (Of course, his wife might be more affirming if he took the time to be with her!) If his primary emotional needs are being met at work, chances are good that there is some work addiction taking place which makes work more appealing than family.

When the work-addicted man finally comes home, his family may not be all that happy to see him. There may be an undercurrent of distrust, anger, resentment, and abandonment because he has been away so much. Before long he may get into a fight with his wife or kids and say, "Enough of this!" It is then far easier to go back to the office where he does not have to face such conflicts. If you asked this man if his family is important to him, he'd say, "Yes! Of course my family is important. Look how hard I work for them. Look what I buy for them. They all have nice cars, good educations, and a financially secure future." Sadly, this man's children do not especially want these things from their father. They would much rather have his heart, his spirit, his time, and his physical presence.

It is a great and special thing when some of a man's emotional needs are met through his work. It is an equally great tragedy when a man allows his work to meet his needs to such an extent that it replaces his family in his heart. When a man's deep emotional needs propel him to replace his family relationships with work and work relationships, he needs to find new ways to meet those needs. He needs to form close, committed relationships with other men so that his deepest needs, unmet in his relationship with his father, can be fulfilled in ways that will not destroy him or his family.

Codependency and Chronic Overwork

Another approval-related consequence of the father-son wound is codependency. Like the work-addicted man, a codependent also uses his work as a way of proving his worth. His method is a bit different, however. He may be so caught up in seeking approval from everyone at work, particularly his boss, that he does not set good boundaries. He is so focused on being loyal to the company at all costs that he cannot set limits on how much he can reasonably accomplish or when his work day should begin or end. He finds himself in a constant state of overcommitment and overwork. Unable to say no, he will try to do more than is humanly possible.

Driven by the hope that he will receive acceptance, approval, and advancement as a reward for his loyalty, the codependent man is often unable to assess what he is actually getting from the company in return for his labor. He is so caught up in seeking approval and pleasing others that he does not watch out for his own welfare. He may work for years without paying much attention to the fact that what he is being paid will never meet his future financial needs. He may labor relentlessly toward a promotion and overlook the fact that only the owner's family members or employees with a particular college degree (that he does not have) are ever placed in such positions.

Ron was a good example of a codependent man. Although his family was active in their church, his father was an alcoholic. When Ron was nine years old, his mother discovered that her husband was having an affair. When she learned this, Ron's father left the family—simply dropping out of Ron's life with no explanation. In reality, Ron's father had emotionally abandoned his family years earlier because of his consuming interests in alcohol and work. Ron never remembers feeling close to his dad. He does remember that his mother was so angry and humiliated by what happened that she stopped going to church and insisted that her children do the same.

As time passed, Ron successfully buried his feelings of abandonment and shame under a load of hard work and accomplishment. After graduating from college, his diligence paid off. He landed a good job with a family-owned company. When Ron joined that company, he felt as if he was part of the family. The little boy within him viewed the owner of the company as the father he never really had. Through hard work and loyalty, Ron advanced quickly through the company and was soon in a position second only to the owner.

But there was a downside to Ron's apparent success and happiness. The little boy within him relentlessly drove him to outperform himself in order to please his employer. His need for acceptance and approval blinded him to the owner's manipulation and control. He could believe nothing but good about his boss, although evidence to the contrary was obvious.

For example, his employer would offer Ron three weeks of vacation if Ron would bring in an additional 15 percent in sales in the coming quarter. Ron would do whatever it took to achieve the goal, but when it came time to receive his reward, his boss would withdraw it. "Cash flow is down," he would say. "I really can't spare you just yet. Can you wait until next month to take the time off?" Ron could not bring himself to disappoint the owner, so he would put off the vacation. He felt more needed, valued, and important when his boss asked him to make these sacrifices.

Ron seemed content to live this way, even though his boss frequently held out an appealing prize and then withdrew it when Ron accomplished the task. Eventually, Ron's work and the toxic nature of his relationship with the owner began taking

a heavy toll on his life. When Ron's health started to deteriorate and his wife threatened to leave him, he began counseling.

For a long time Ron could not understand how it was possible
for him to think so clearly and make such wise business decisions,
yet give in when he faced a confrontation with his boss. He began
to recognize the real issue when he asked for a Friday off to go on
a Boy Scout camping trip with his son. He had just put in an
eighty-hour week and had landed a major new contract that
would open up entirely new avenues of business and income for
the company. Ron's boss still refused to give him a day off, and
Ron missed an important time with his son.

When Ron saw the sadness in his boy's eyes, he began to
realize that he had disappointed his son in this way many times
before. For the first time, Ron began to feel some of that
sadness and to understand his need to set boundaries with his
boss. He decided to seek additional counseling and began
attending a Codependents Anonymous group.

As his recovery continued, Ron realized how the wounds of
his father-son relationship had caused him to be out of control
in his relationship with his boss. With the help of his sponsor,
Ron began writing down how he would set boundaries with his
boss. As he set those boundaries and cut back on his work time,
Ron realized that his codependence had allowed his boss to
ignore Ron's need for an assistant. Ron was literally doing the
work of more than two people! As expected, Ron's boss did not
like it when Ron started recognizing his own needs and setting
boundaries. He became critical and angry. One day he even
threatened Ron, "Either you work to meet the needs of this
company as you did before, or you will lose your job!"

At one time in his life, these words would have devastated
Ron. They still were frightening to him, but now he could talk
over the situation with his sponsor, his counselor, and his men's
group. Armed with their perspective and support, Ron went to
his boss and reaffirmed the clear boundaries he had set with
him. He calmly explained that he was no longer willing to work

the long hours he had before and that he needed at least one more person in his department in order to accomplish his work effectively. He also reminded his boss that he was a highly skilled and valuable employee and that if his employer wanted to fire him, he had no problem with that.

Ron did not lose his job. He was able to hire the additional employees he needed and is maintaining his boundaries at work. As he continues to heal and grow, however, Ron is thinking about starting his own business. He has become increasingly tired of the dysfunction in his present company and would like the opportunity to put into practice the values and attitudes he believes will lead to success.

Ron is not the only man who has struggled with codependence in his efforts to gain approval in the workplace. I see a bit of codependence in David when Saul offered him his daughter, Michal, in marriage. David did not feel worthy of receiving such a great reward, and Saul responded by demanding nothing less than 100 Philistine foreskins as the price for his daughter. David did not even consider the possibility that Saul had named that price because he hoped David would die in the effort. Anxious to feel worthy and oblivious to the unreasonableness of Saul's demand, David went out and brought back not 100, but 200 foreskins! (1 Samuel 18:20-27).

The codependence that affected Ron in the workplace also affects some men in Christian service. Some missionaries, for example, have devoted their working years to service on foreign mission fields. Dedicated to the Lord and the organizations they serve, some of these men have never discussed their retirement needs with their mission board. They have given years of service under the assumption that when they could no longer serve effectively, the mission organization would take care of them. Not until they return home to retire do they realize that they have no resources on which to live.

Pastors, too, must deal with this issue. A recent survey of pastors indicated that 90 percent of them work more than forty-six hours a week. A frightening 80 percent of them also believe their ministry adversely affects their families. Sadly, 70 percent of pastors say they do not have anyone they would consider to be a close friend.[3]

It is good that some men are willing to devote their lives to Christian service. However, a man who "serves the Lord" to his own detriment or to the detriment of his family may be doing so out of a deep desire to earn recognition and approval from his earthly father rather than out of his commitment to serve his Heavenly Father. I encourage Christian men who desire to serve their Heavenly Father to feel their grief and deal with the wounds in their relationships with their earthly fathers. Then they will be set free to truly serve God.

Unrealistic Expectations

A man's expectations for his career and the success he achieves in it are affected by the kind of relationship he has with his father. Throughout every stage of life a man needs relationships with older men who will initiate him, support him, guide him, train him, and bring him along through the challenges of life. Life is never as easy, rewarding, or idyllic as a boy dreams it will be. Part of the father's responsibility is to help his son face the harsh reality of life and to teach him how to deal successfully with life.

Allow me to share with you an example of how I introduced my son, Ben, to some of life's harder truths. One of Ben's earliest jobs was to deliver realtors' brochures house-to-house. Once a month he would deliver two thousand brochures and be paid a nickel each. As he began this venture, I talked to him about the reality of business and the need to set aside some profit to cover overhead. I explained that since he carried the brochures in his backpack, that was his overhead. I also pointed out that his backpack was starting to fall apart and that he would need to set aside some money to buy another one.

At the time he ignored me. But a few months later, when he had more brochures to deliver, he showed me his torn backpack and explained how hard it would be to carry the brochures by hand rather than in his pack. Then he asked if he could borrow some money for a new backpack. It was hard for me to do so, but I said, "No. I will not lend you the money."

Was he upset with me! When he got paid, he went out and bought an expensive leather backpack. I knew he had bought an expensive one because he was angry with me. When he showed it to me I said, "That is a very nice backpack, Ben. You spent a lot of money on it. It's your money, but buying this backpack means you have twenty dollars less to spend on other things you enjoy. Eventually this one will wear out, just like the nylon ones do." A day later, Ben exchanged the expensive backpack for a less expensive one and was pleased to have twenty dollars left over.

This incident taught Ben several important principles. He learned that it is important to anticipate needs and plan for the future—and that if he did not, no one was going to bail him out. He also learned that if he did not have the money he needed, he would have to make do with what he had. And he learned to think carefully before making a purchase. In a small way, this illustrates how a father can help his son deal with the realities of life.

The father's objective in providing reality checks for his son is not to kill his child's dreams, but to help him learn to make the right decisions in pursuing those dreams. Now Ben is older and would like to have a Toyota four-wheel-drive pickup truck. I've agreed that it would be a nice thing to have. When he looked in the newspaper and told me how expensive they were, I said, "These are hard decisions to make. People sometimes buy expensive things and have to spend all their time working to support those things. Sometimes people have to give up other things that are also important." I then gave him our insurance agent's phone number so he could find out what the insurance would cost. (I could have told him how much it was, but in his mind my information would have seemed inaccurate or an exaggeration!) After he called the agent, he came back to me and said, "Dad! Do you know how much that insurance costs?"

"Yeah," I said, "It's a bummer, isn't it?"

This kind of input from the father or other men is essential to a young man growing into adulthood. Without it, a young man may grow up with a very unrealistic idea of who he is and what he is able to do. He may become a perpetual student who is great at acquiring knowledge but unable to take the risks of turning that knowledge into a successful career. He may become a man who forever changes jobs. Moving from job to job, he may never be satisfied for more than a few months with what he is doing or the people with whom he works. He may be fired repeatedly and forced to change jobs because he does not have what it takes to do a job well over the long term.

Alan, a man in his forties, is an example of a man who missed out on the guidance and accountability a father can provide. He was deeply wounded by his father's death when he was just nine years old. Alan is brilliant. He reads widely and can carry on an intelligent conversation on almost any subject. He has taken all kinds of courses and amassed who-knows-how-many credits, but he has never been successful in his career. He does not have a usable degree, nor can he keep a job for more than a few months. He is always months behind in his bills and has never been able to support his family.

What is his problem? It is not lack of ability; he can sell, invent, and design. It is not that he cannot get a job; he can always do that. In fact, people love him for the first month. After that they learn to hate him. He becomes arrogant, self-centered, sloppy, and does not follow through on his assignments. People soon learn that they cannot count on him, so he is turned out on the street again.

This pattern goes back to the wound he suffered when his father died. When that happened, no other man—no grandfather, uncle, or man in the church—stepped forward to be there for him. No man was there to help him deal with his loss or to nurture and guide his fantastic intellect into a productive resource. No man was there to make him accountable in dealing with life. When Alan reached late adolescence, no man was there to say, "I will support you emotionally and teach you what I can, but you need to be responsible enough to pay your bills on your own."

Alan, who had several older female relatives, turned toward women to meet his needs. These relatives, who felt sorry for him and gave him money, still bail him out. So he has never learned to be responsible or productive in his career.

When sons are not nurtured by their fathers through the early stages of life, they do not have a realistic picture of what it takes to be successful. Deep inside, many young men are looking for someone to say, "You're the greatest. You're wonderful!" They expect to start out making $50,000 a year. They have no idea that it may take years of low-paying, unfulfilling, menial, tedious work to achieve their ultimate career goals. They have little or no tolerance for jobs that are not what they ultimately want, so they end up frustrated, angry, and depressed at the realities of life.

Fathers play an incredibly important role in helping their sons develop successful, rewarding, and well-balanced careers. When a man is greatly wounded in his relationship with his father, he is also greatly hindered in his ability to meet his career goals. The father-son wound may drive a man to work addiction. It may cause him to be outwardly successful but inwardly destructive. It may cause him to imprison himself in a difficult and unrewarding career. It can even lead a man to fail to develop a career at all. When a man deals with his deep woundedness, however, he can begin making real choices and real progress in his career.

CHAPTER 6

The Impact of the Father Wound on a Man's Spiritual Life

Although one might be tempted to believe that a man's spiritual life would be untouched by the harmful effects of the father-son wound, it does not happen that way. A man's wounded relationship with his father impacts his spiritual life just as strongly as it impacts any other part of his existence. The veil of emotional detachment through which most men experience life severely inhibits their development of a vibrant spiritual lifestyle. Furthermore, a man's personal relationship with God often mimics his relationship with his father.

The overall result of father wound on the religious life of most men is that they tend to be spiritually passive and inactive. They may come to church, but they are not really there. They may hear a sermon intellectually, but its message may never penetrate their hearts enough to make a difference in their lives. They may serve as ushers and shake people's hands before and after the service or as elders who make financial and policy decisions for the church, but they often cannot make themselves connect with what church is really about. They can't connect enough to be fully involved with heart, mind, and soul.

The Father Wound Contributes to a Growing Spiritual Vacuum

Despite the fact that men dominate the pastoral staffs of most churches, a masculine vacuum exists within the church today. Men may attend services, but tend to stay on the periphery, not really having the heart and passion to actively minister to others. The most disciplined men may read Scripture daily and be able to factually discuss the Bible, but they rarely feel the emotion, intensity, and spiritual impact of what Scripture reveals about God's dealings with humanity. Lacking a feeling connection in their relationship with God, most men feel inadequate to be the spiritual leaders they know they should be, so they feel shamed. They tend to withdraw from the church, leaving even less male leadership for the next generation.

Consider, for example, how many men in your church are Sunday school teachers. In most churches a boy can attend church every Sunday of his life, from infancy until he graduates from high school, and never have a male Sunday school teacher. Try to identify the men in your church (other than the pastoral staff) who lead Bible studies or initiate church programs for men. If your church is like most churches, women either design or run a high percentage of church programs.

The fact is, today's Christian church is primarily a feminine church. By saying this, I do not mean to imply that I am anti-feminine. However, I must ask, "Where are the men?" Where are the men who are spiritually alive? Who have a fire in their bellies—a passion to grow toward God, a passion to grow as men, and a passion to grow toward other men? Who are willing to take bold risks in their faith? Where are the men who will take action in sharing the gospel of Christ? Who will live out their faith through active involvement in the Christian community and through active outreach to those outside the church community?

The church desperately needs the involvement of such men, yet they are difficult to find. For generations, men have been wounded by the lack of male leadership and modeling of spiritual truth by older men. Consequently, men are greatly shamed when they realize that they should be spiritual leaders, teachers, and models, yet have no idea how to assume those roles. Many men would rather abandon the church (either physically or emotionally) than deal with these feelings of shame and inadequacy.

Our Spiritual Expectations Are Shaming

The truth is, our traditional expectations of a man's spiritual leadership are in themselves shaming. No one would pick a man out of the crowd, put him in an operating room with a patient, instruments, and support staff, and expect him to successfully perform a triple bypass operation. A man needs education, training, and supervised experience before he can perform heart surgery with any degree of success. Within the church, however, there is an underlying expectation that every man, with no training whatsoever, ought to be a masterful spiritual leader. This expectation is neither realistic nor fair.

Many men feel as if they have to be biblical scholars before they have anything significant to offer to the Christian community. The fear of failing to meet this expectation keeps men on the outside of church life and ministry, reinforcing the masculine vacuum that exists. For instance, a man may be afraid to become involved in a Sunday school class for boys because he thinks he has to teach some great theological truth. He may not realize that the real challenge for a boys' Sunday school teacher is to contain an incredible amount of energy in one room for a specified period of time! Of course, a man needs some knowledge of Scripture and needs to prepare what he intends to teach, but he does not have to be a magnificent Bible scholar to teach a group of boys. He can teach effectively simply by knowing how to connect with them and sharing in a meaningful way what he has learned about God through Scripture and through his life experiences.

Unfortunately, it is hard for men to recognize that no matter who they are or what skills they have, they can have an active ministry through the church. Consider Bob, who had always felt a little bit ashamed because he was a builder and woodworker and did not have a college degree. Many adults in his church attached a high amount of status to advanced degrees and frequently talked about what college they and their kids attended. Bob felt as if he did not have much to talk about with them because no one seemed to value the kinds of trade skills he had.

Bob's attitude toward himself and what he had to offer others in his church began to change after he spent some time with an uncle. This uncle, who was also a builder, reminisced about Bob's grandfather, who had been a builder too. Through these talks with his uncle, Bob began to feel a sense of pride in the fact that he was part of several generations of builders. He began to be more expressive and involved with men at church. Eventually, several friends asked him if he would teach them some basic woodworking skills. He enthusiastically agreed and asked the men to bring their teenage sons along with them.

Their time together was fantastic. Two fathers and their sons learned about woodworking from an older man and loved it. Bob was able to help these fathers enjoy a close experience with their sons, something he had never experienced with his father. Since that first day of woodworking, the teenagers have come back to spend time with Bob in his shop. Because Bob is a deep, feeling man, these boys—just by being with him—will gain a stronger image of what Christian manhood is all about and will grow in their understanding of God.

This is just one example of how a man can have an important and active spiritual involvement in the Christian community. A man's spiritual leadership in the home and church involves far more than his ability to lead a Bible study or to share the gospel message through a tract. A man can share his expertise and experiences in a wide variety of ways. When a man cares enough to share what he has inside with another man, boy, or young man, he touches a deep need in that individual. It helps him experience a little more of what it means to be a Christian man and helps him understand a little more of what it means to be loved by God.

After all, a man does not become a godly Christian the moment he is saved, and a man does not learn how to be a godly person on his own. He learns this through the active involvement of his father and other men who teach and model spiritual leadership through everyday living. When his father and other men are not spiritually alive and active in the church, a man is deeply wounded.

Like many men of my generation and of generations before me, I have felt this woundedness. No men actively participated in my spiritual life while I was growing up. My Sunday school teachers were women. I am thankful for the role they played in my spiritual development. I am thankful that they answered my questions and taught me the importance of Bible study and prayer, but the absence of men who were actively involved in my spiritual growth subtly communicated to me that church was women's work. It taught me that church was less important than making a living and providing for a family. It also taught me that it was normal for a man to be passive and distant in his relationship with God and His church. This is certainly not what masculine Christian spirituality is all about.

When Men Are Emotionally Detached, They Are Spiritually Detached

It is a dreadful thing to say, but the spiritual life of many men goes no deeper than sitting in a pew on Sunday, finding the right Bible verses, and singing a few hymns. Often there is little carry over of spiritual principles into a man's daily life. I believe that a man's tendency toward emotional detachment from what is happening inside him and around him greatly contributes to an empty, fruitless spiritual life. A man who has numbed himself to his emotions has also numbed himself to his spiritual feelings. He can know that God loves him but unless he has experienced what it feels like to be loved by another person, it is incredibly hard for him to feel loved by God. Under these conditions, it is impossible to live a life that is directed by that love.

Patrick Arnold expresses the problem of emotional and spiritual detachment well: "I hurt inside as I see the great divorce that has developed over the generations between men and Christian spirituality. I hurt for the men that have lost the close contact with God that a healthy religiosity can nurture. This is an alienation that affects me personally as well as most men."[1]

Solomon is a good example of an emotionally and spiritually detached man. His life illustrates the divorce between spiritual knowledge and spiritual living. Solomon was filled with God's wisdom. He had not only been taught about God, but had experienced two personal encounters with Him (1 Kings 11:9). One has to wonder how much of what Solomon experienced touched him on a feeling level, for there is ample evidence of emotional detachment throughout his life. He appears to have been an alcoholic, one of humankind's favorite ways to numb inner feelings (Proverbs 23:29–35). One could safely conclude that Solomon was a compulsive worker (Ecclesiastes 2:4–6), a compulsive spender (Ecclesiastes 2:7–8), and a compulsive student (1 Kings 4:29–34). His acquisition of 700 wives and 300 concubines (1 Kings 11:3) could easily lead one to conclude that he buried his inner feelings through compulsive sexual activity.

Solomon's writings, which include three thousand proverbs and more than a thousand songs (1 Kings 4:32), also illustrate his spiritual detachment. Although these writings show a broad knowledge of God, they show little evidence of a deep, feeling relationship with God. If you were to compare, for example, Solomon's proverbs with David's psalms you would see that Solomon's proverbs convey spiritual knowledge but lack the passion and vital, personal relationship with God that dominates David's psalms. About the only time we see evidence of an intimate, passionate relationship with God is in Solomon's prayer at the dedication of the temple (1 Kings 8:15–61).

The tragedy of Solomon's life is that, despite his personal encounters with God, despite God's gift of incomparable wisdom, and despite his leadership position as king of God's holy nation, Solomon could not maintain his spiritual commitment to God. By the end of his life, Solomon had completely lost this spiritual connection. His detachment from God, in turn, had a devastating impact on his sons and the nation of Israel.

What was the source of Solomon's tragic emotional detachment? I believe it can be traced, at least in part, to his relationship with his father David. When he was king of Israel, David's family life indicates a certain amount of emotional detachment. This is particularly evident in his lack of responsiveness to his daughter Tamar's rape by her half-brother Amnon. This emotional detachment is what he modeled to his son Solomon. David's extramarital affair also wounded Solomon. Through this affair David modeled that it was preferable to turn to women as a source of comfort and support rather than to men. Solomon's choices in life provide ample evidence of the deep wounds these experiences left on his heart.

I do not believe the father-son wound has any less of an impact on the spiritual lives of men today than it did in Solomon's time. Contrary to what many Christians seem to believe, dramatic spiritual experiences are not sufficient to maintain godly Christian living for a lifetime. If a man is to continue to live under God's direction, spiritual truth must touch the depths of his heart. Most men cannot be touched deeply until they feel the pain of their wounded hearts and reach out for healing.

Too many men, too many Christian leaders, try to live on the basis of their past spiritual experience and fail. This is why we see men whom God has used greatly plunge into compulsive behaviors that destroy their ministries and defame God's name. No amount of spiritual teaching or number of experiences can erase the reality of a man's emotional and spiritual woundedness. Unless a man deals with his father-son wound, he remains unable to connect with the emotional and spiritual reality with his heart. When a man is not emotionally connected, he will not feel loved by God. If he does not feel God's love deep in his heart, he cannot truly live the Christian life.

A man who is detached from his feelings cannot feel the needs of his own Christian community. He has no feeling for the boy in the single-parent family who has no contact with his father. He has no compassion for the elderly widow in his church who perhaps has a bad roof or a home that needs a paint job but has only enough money for essentials. He has no feeling for the father in his church who has been laid off and can no longer pay the mortgage on his home. He feels no need to call the man, take him out to lunch, and encourage him as he searches for another job. He has no concern for the teenager in the youth group who, as he wades through the turmoil of his teenage years, needs the security and stability of older men who are involved in his life. He does not care about the young boy in Sunday school who is hungry to soak up anything an older man who deeply loves God has to offer.

When Men are Emotionally Connected, They Are Spiritually Activated

When a man begins to deal with his own woundedness and becomes more emotionally connected, he becomes spiritually alive as well. When Scripture finally gets to a man's heart, he becomes spiritually motivated. He begins to feel what Christian living is all about, and it changes his life. This kind of transformation was especially evident in the life of Steve, a client who first came to me because he could not remain sober for any length of time.

For several generations the men in Steve's family had been work addicts and alcoholics. The women in the family went to church, but the men never seemed to have time for church activities. Steve was an out-of-control drinker, just as his father and grandfather had been, until a family crisis forced him to begin making changes. He then committed himself to attending ninety Alcoholics Anonymous meetings in ninety days because he knew it would take that amount of concentrated effort to make a change.

By working through the twelve steps of Alcoholics Anonymous, Steve became aware of something bigger than himself that enabled him to stay sober one day at a time. He started to identify and feel his inner woundedness. This discovery enabled him to start making an emotional connection with his wife and kids. For the first time in his life, he also started making a spiritual connection with God.

Meanwhile, one of his sons had become an altar boy. I suggested to Steve that it would mean a lot to his son if he would go to church and see him serve as an altar boy. Steve hung his head, telling me he was too ashamed to go to church. When I asked him why, he responded, "I wouldn't know what to do if I had to look up something in the Bible."

I'd never heard anyone say that before, but I sat down next to him and showed him how to find verses in the Bible. Then I shared the "big secret" with him. "The truth is," I said, "hardly anybody knows where *all* of the books of the Bible are anyway! Sooner or later, most of us have to look up one in the Table of Contents!"

He laughed and could hardly believe me, but I assured him that what I said was true. I also led him through the Four Spiritual Laws and encouraged him to go through the booklet again and make his own decision. Shortly afterward, Steve decided to ask Christ into his life. His sobriety increased and he started going to church regularly. Now he goes to church about a half hour early so he can meditate before the worship service begins. He reads the hymns and Scripture selections for the service and thinks about them. "You know, Earl," he said recently. "I don't know why more people aren't in church before it starts. It's so quiet. It's the best time all week to focus on my relationship with God. I have to do it because it helps me stay sober and maintain conscious contact with God."

It has been fascinating to work with Steve. He spends time every day praying for his father, even as he is healing from the wounds he suffered in his relationship with him. As Steve works through his father-son wound, he has become more able to be open and involved with his wife and sons. He has explained to his sons that he is an alcoholic, has talked with them about the things he has done to them, and asked for their forgiveness. He has also explained that he is now always available to talk with them about whatever they need to discuss. After this his teenage sons really opened up to him. Since he has made amends with his wife and sons, they have all experienced a closeness and trust that was not possible before.

Dealing with the woundedness in his relationship with his father has opened the way for Steve to experience a depth of spiritual vitality that many men who have gone to church for a lifetime have yet to discover. This is possible because Steve is no longer an emotionally and spiritually detached man. He is a good example of how a man can change, of how an emotionally and spiritually detached man can begin to really live out the Christian life.

Like Father, Like God

A man's relationship with his father has a tremendous bearing on his personal relationship with God. When a bond exists between father and son, the son will find it easier to trust his father's spirituality and to model his father's spiritual life.

If a man's relationship with his earthly father has been marked by woundedness, he will find it difficult to know how to expect anything different in his relationship with God. In fact, a little boy's first image of God the Father reflects the image of his earthly father. A strong emotional connection between father and son, makes it easier for the son to feel spiritually connected with God, but if no emotional bridge exists, the son may feel as though God is distant and disinterested.

Consider these common examples of how a man's relationship with God mirrors his relationship with his father:

- If a man's father has been unpredictable or moody, made promises he did not keep, or failed to support him when he needed it, a man does not know what he can count on in his relationship with his Heavenly Father.
- If a man's father has been critical, judgmental, difficult to please, or cruel, a man will tend to view God as a harsh taskmaster who is just waiting for an excuse to punish him.
- If a man's father has been shaming or demanded perfection, a man will feel hopelessly inadequate before God, compelled to do as much as he can "for God," yet feeling guilty for never doing enough.
- If a man's father has been passive when action was appropriate, a man will have a hard time trusting God to play an active role in his life.
- If a man's father had a strong, macho personality, showed no compassion and denied or minimized pain, a man will find it hard to believe that God is compassionate and cares deeply about his pain, his struggles, or his fears.

Clearly, all of the emotions that are wrapped up in a man's relationship with his father are also wrapped up in his relationship with God. When healing for those issues begins to take place, a man will experience God differently and feel His presence more deeply.

This healing process was apparent in Steve's life. As Steve began his recovery from alcoholism, he had to deal with the reality of his father's emotional, physical, and spiritual abuse. His father's abuse left his son with so much shame that it was hard for him to even walk into a church. Since Steve did not know how to act or behave in church, he was terrified of what might happen if he did something wrong. This overwhelming fear of God and church was rooted in Steve's fear of his father, who would explode in rage any time Steve was less than perfect.

With this knowledge of Steve's father, it is not at all difficult to understand why going to church and opening his heart to Christ was such a big step for Steve. I do not believe he could have taken this step and maintained a growing relationship with Christ if he had not connected with his father-son wound.

Hope for the Christian Community

I believe that tremendous change must and can take place among men in the Christian community. I look forward to the day when Christian men will feel their spirituality deep in their hearts, when men will have experienced enough healing in their relationships with their earthly fathers to experience an intensely personal relationship with their Heavenly Father. I look forward to the day when Christian men will rise up in their masculine strength and make a positive difference in the church and the world.

I believe Christian men can fulfill this vision. When I was a teenager growing up on a southern Minnesota farm, I witnessed what a united masculine community can do. The incident I would like to share with you is not overtly spiritual, but it conveys a strong image of active, masculine spirituality.

Toward the end of one summer, a farmer on a neighboring farm became very sick. His health was often mentioned during discussions at the places men gathered to talk—the grain elevator, the café, and the service station. Everyone knew he would not be able to harvest his corn and plow his fields to prepare them for the next spring's planting. Before long, a date was set when the entire farming community would descend on that man's farm to get the job done.

Early on the designated day, two or three combines, four or five tractors with plows, and men with trucks and wagons to haul the corn drove up to the farm of the man in need. The giant combines began their slow, relentless advance across the corn fields, pulling and shelling ears row after row. Soon I could see the hoppers filling with mounds of golden corn. Then, one by one, the trucks pulled up underneath the combine's unloading augers that spilled a golden stream into each waiting truck. Neither truck nor combine ever stopped. They continued helping the man in need, driven by the urgency of the coming cold weather and snow that would destroy the crop. When the combines and trucks had passed, tractors pulling stalk choppers, disks, and plows followed, readying the ground for the next spring's planting.

I remember feeling like I belonged in the world of men that day. I can still see men waving and smiling at each other as they passed in the fields. I can still hear the roar of the diesel engines and see the belch of black exhaust when the pulling got tough. I can still feel the ground tremble under the strength of all those men and their machines working together to harvest another man's crop. I remember stopping for the noon meal, listening to men laugh and tell stories—some of which were about times past when their fathers helped neighbors in a similar way.

Although that event took place more than twenty-five years ago, I still feel an incredible sense of participating in something very significant that day. I will never forget the strength of that camaraderie and the confidence deep in my heart that the same kind of help would be there for me if I ever needed it.

Without really knowing it at the time, I caught a glimpse of what masculine spirituality can be. I saw what it means for one man to help another, and I experienced something of God's love that I had not known before.

I remember that day with a certain sadness too. The strength of masculine spirituality I witnessed was not as easy to see in everyday life. There was an underlying sense of caring among the men of that community, but no outward, direct expression of that care was ever made unless a crisis forced it out. Most of those men believed in Christ, but theirs was a silent, private faith—just as their emotions were silent and private. Men tended to stay on the periphery of church life, indirectly communicating to their sons that the things of God were important in the world of women but not in the world of men.

Deep inside my heart I know these men desired a strong spirituality, but that they lacked a way to express it openly. This is one of the sad legacies of the father-son wound: generations of spiritually passive men who have never found the fire in their belly that moves them to become active participants in the Christian community; who can touch the hearts of the wounded, poor, and widowed as Christ did. But this legacy can be changed when men take the scary, painful steps to grieve for their wounds and seek healing through the company of other men.

CHAPTER 7

Masculine Growth Begins With Healing Relationships

Masculine growth is a real and challenging process. It takes integrity for a man to admit woundedness. It takes great courage for a man to face the pain of the father-son wound and deal with the deep, unresolved issues in his life. It takes tremendous strength for him to recognize that he is vulnerable, not the invincible "man of steel" he has trained himself to be. For these reasons and more, it is not easy for a man to begin the recovery process.

No man wants to feel this kind of grief. It hurts all the way through. The tears that come are beyond control—normal defenses suddenly do not work. For a time, a man in recovery is out of control, crying about things he has never cried about and feeling things he has never felt.

This is not an easy experience to enter into. No matter at what age a man starts dealing with these issues, he has spent his whole life defining what it means to be masculine. When he takes steps toward healing, everything he thought he knew about being a man is suddenly up for grabs. This uncertainty makes him feel insecure, maybe even a little bit crazy.

Once a man takes steps toward masculine growth, however, he knows he is moving in the right direction. Once he opens the door, there is no turning back. He may be in for quite a ride, but the reward of discovering a newfound sense of what it means to be a man, of sharing truly deep relationships and experiencing a spirituality that touches his very soul, is worth the risk.

Growth Means Becoming Connected With the Little Boy Inside

Inside every man is a child who still feels all the emotions associated with the deep wound in the father-son relationship. Too many adult men have not connected emotionally with this little boy. Some men, who have disassociated themselves from the child-like part of their nature, may appear to be very "adult." They are controlled, not playful, and are unable to laugh freely or have fun. Other men are possessed by the whims of the child-like part of themselves, and seem very immature and self-centered. They pursue their own pleasures to the exclusion of their families or fail to take on their responsibilities as fathers and husbands. Both types of men have not connected with the little boys within them. As a result, they live as victims of their father-son wound, completely unaware of it. As we've seen in previous chapters, that wound affects their work, their friendships, their family life, their community life, and their relationship with God.

For a man to begin healing from his father-son wound, he must reconnect with the little boy inside. When he does that, he builds an emotional bridge between his adult self and his feelings. He is then able to deal with the sadness, grief, anger, and other deep emotions related to his father-son wound.

Consider how Dave changed when he connected with the child inside. Dave began counseling because of deep depression and recurrent panic attacks. A kind and likable man, he was somewhat passive and had difficulty expressing his feelings.

One of the first things I asked him about was his family. Dave was the youngest of three boys. He was born rather late in his parents' life, so his next oldest brother was ten years older than he was. As Dave grew up, he rarely heard from his brothers. His father held a variety of jobs—everything from being a cowboy to serving in the merchant marine. Although his mother was protective of her youngest son, the whole family was rather disconnected and detached. No one had much of anything to say to anyone else, and no one shared their feelings openly.

After learning about Dave's family background, I asked him to close his eyes and picture himself as a little boy. He immediately burst into tears and began sobbing. Just by imagining himself as a little boy, he felt the grief, emptiness, and loneliness he had experienced when he was young. I then asked him to imagine his adult self stepping toward the little boy and holding him close. This process brought about even deeper sobs, which was disconcerting for him.

Dave was surprised by his emotional reaction. It did not match up with his view of masculinity. Dave believed that big boys were not supposed to cry, that Jesus was supposed to wash away all the pain, and that men were supposed to handle their problems on their own. Dave's image of tough, self-sufficient masculinity shattered as the reality of his inner pain burst through his conscious experience. He came face to face with the overwhelming sadness and grief of a little boy who, although he knew his father loved him, had never felt the warmth of that love or felt the depth of his father's care.

As Dave walked through this valley of grief, he began to make sense out of his panic attacks and depression. He could feel the grief of what he, as a young boy, had missed in his relationship with his dad. He was able to mourn the loss of his father, who died while Dave was in his early twenties. He felt the sadness, confusion, and fear of not having a dad to talk to

when he married and, later, when he became a father. He
realized that although he had a successful career and was
approaching retirement, he felt very young, fragile, and afraid.

By connecting with the little boy inside, Dave connected
with the deep wound he had suffered in his relationship with
his father. This is where the healing of the father-son wound
begins. It is important to realize, however, that this is just the
beginning of healing, not the whole process. The process of
healing continues as a man deepens his relationships with
other men and with God.

Growth Isn't Achieved Alone

One thing that is particularly hard about feeling and healing the woundedness in his relationship with his father is that
a man cannot do it alone. Although he may have received a
lifetime of messages that say a "real man" does it on his own,
the business of connecting with his inner feelings and healing
is accomplished in the company of other men.

It is not always easy for a man to find the men he needs for
support. A man's pastor, whom he may have admired for years,
may not understand what a man in recovery is going through.
Unless a man is very fortunate, his father will not understand
it either. Even his best friend does not understand unless the
two of them are going through it at the same time. So a man
may feel very lonely and scared until he connects with men who
do understand and are willing to support him.

If this is your situation, the men you need to talk with are
those who believe that being vulnerable—talking about worries
or fears—is something vital to manhood. They will not see this
kind of openness as a weakness or a spiritual defect, but as
positive growth. They know that becoming a man is a lifelong
challenge and that the way is not mapped out for any man.
They know that you, like every man, are covering new ground
all along the way and do not always know which way to turn.

The concept of men sharing with men is nothing new. Primitive societies, such as certain tribes in Africa, the aboriginal cultures of Australia, and American Indian tribes, have long legacies of initiation and training. In these cultures, men traditionally do not function solely on their own, but as part of the whole male community. The community of men hunts together, fights together, and actively brings the younger men into its circle. The camaraderie, support, and strength of a united community of men (and women) is essential to the survival of the culture.

In Scripture we also see evidence of the strength and support male relationships can provide. Some men seem specifically guided by God to carry out their lives alone, for the most part without close relationships with other men. These men include Abraham, Elijah, Joseph, and John the Baptist. It seems that some men, such as Lot, Samson and Jonah, would have benefitted greatly if they had experienced close, supportive relationships with godly men. Some men clearly were better people because of their close male relationships. David, the man who loved God, was one of these.

For part of his life, David enjoyed the covenant friendship of Jonathan. These men were powerful warriors, yet were very close spiritually and emotionally. They shared their deepest concerns with one another and neither was afraid to risk his life for the other.

There is no evidence that David's son, Solomon, ever had such a friend. Even Solomon's great wisdom and dramatic spiritual experiences did not fill the loneliness he felt inside. In the emptiness of his life, Solomon wrote:

> Two are better than one,
> because they have a good return for their work:
> If one falls down,
> his friend can help him up.
> But pity the man who falls
> and has no one to help him up!

Also, if two lie down together, they will keep warm.
But how can one keep warm alone?
Though one may be overpowered,
two can defend themselves.
A cord of three strands is not quickly broken.

                                        Ecclesiastes 4:9–12

One has to wonder how the course of Solomon's life might have been different if there had been even one close friend to stand by him, encourage him, and comfort him during his struggles. If Solomon had had a close friend, perhaps he would not have needed a thousand wives and concubines. Perhaps he would have worshiped the one true God throughout his life rather than abandoning Him to worship a host of lifeless idols.

I think it is helpful for Christian men to think about the relationships between men in Scripture and to consider the truths their examples reveal. As I look at the relationships between men in the Bible, I see clear examples of the great benefits to be had through close, supportive, male relationships. I find it interesting that even Jesus did not work by Himself. He needed no one to do miracles for Him or to speak for Him, yet He chose to minister in the close company of twelve chosen men. They learned from Him as He shared with them. When it came time for Him to send His disciples out into the world, He sent them in twos, not alone. In His hour of personal need, Jesus asked three of those men to be with Him in the Garden of Gethsemane during the night He was betrayed.

Relationships With Women Don't Nurture Masculine Growth

As we have seen, it is easy for men who long for meaningful relationships to seek out relationships with women rather than with men. However, a boy can only become a man through relationships with other men. Only men can welcome a boy into the world of men. Only men can share their struggles,

failures, responsibilities, and dreams, thereby showing a younger man how to live as a man in each new stage of life. Only
men can guide, encourage, and nurture a man along the path
of masculine growth.

This truth is difficult for mothers and their boys to accept.
Often a mother will see the deep wound in her son's life. She
will perceive that something is lacking in her son's relationship
with his father and will try to fill that void with extra portions
of mothering. In response, the son finds it easy to gravitate
toward his mother because her warmth and sensitivity feel
good to him. Most often, no matter how well intended the
mother's attempt to fill the gap, the boy's emotional movement
toward his mother leads to a toxic, codependent relationship
between mother and son. This is very wounding to the son.

Obviously the single-parent mother is in a tough spot. Try as
she might, there is no way she can fill all of her son's emotional
needs. The situation is even more desperate if the son's father
does not fulfill his emotional responsibility to spend time with his
son and be involved in his life. A boy who is over-mothered and
under-fathered has real problems. That is why the relationship
between a mother and her teenage son can become explosive. A
mother may do everything that she knows is right to do in raising
her son, yet when he reaches his teens he may ignore her, be
disrespectful to her, or even become violent.

What is happening in situations like this is that the son is
trying to break away from his emotional dependence on his
mother, which at some point he needs to do. But he cannot
make a successful break unless he has contact with older men
who take an interest in him and bring him along as he grows
into manhood. A functioning masculine community within the
church can fill this need. If such a community of men existed,
many godly men would be available to pick up where fathers
have failed.

All boys, whether they are raised in single-parent or two-
parent homes, need to make an emotional break with their

mothers. This emotional break does not mean that young men no longer love or care about their mothers. It means that they need to separate themselves from their mothers emotionally and begin to deal with their own issues. They need to see the world through their own eyes rather than through their mothers' eyes. It means mothers have to make a conscious—and yes, painful—effort to let go of their sons and allow them to become men. This emotional break sets sons free to become part of the community of men.

It is not easy for a son to make this emotional break with his mother. He certainly cannot do it alone. It takes solid relationships with a number of men for the break to be successful. A son not only needs a relationship with his father, but relationships with uncles, grandfathers, and other men who are close to the family in order to leave the world of childhood and enter the world of manhood. Consider the roles that each of these types of men can play in a man's ongoing maturity.

A Boy Needs a Relationship With His Grandfather

Every boy has a place in his soul that only a grandfather can fill. The grandfather is usually the first older man (other than the father, of course) to whom a boy becomes connected. When an older man speaks, he speaks from the well of a lifetime of experience. Having made it through the rigors of life, he can cry deeply, laugh deeply, and love deeply. A grandfather who has lived a rich and passionate life automatically seems to command respect from his family. He imparts a stability and wisdom that only he can give. As a true patriarch, a grandfather who has achieved a balance in the emotional, spiritual, and physical aspects of life has much to give to the younger members of his family. I'm not envisioning a man who walks on water, but I want to emphasize the solid, masculine influence a grandfather can have on a boy who is maturing into manhood. All men need an infusion of the strength, fullness, and depth that sharing in the life of an older man can provide.

For many boys, such a wonderful relationship has been lost. Many grandfathers, for example, do not understand that God designed children with a deep need to share intimate experiences with their grandparents. A grandfather may not realize that his grandson hungers for such a relationship. This relationship should include more than holiday visits, although those gatherings of the generations are certainly significant.

Grandfathers must realize that, just as fathers need to build an emotional bridge to their sons, grandfathers need to build an emotional bridge to their grandsons. That emotional bridge does not exist on its own. *Grandfathers must take steps to build it by being involved in their grandsons' lives*. Perhaps the greatest gift a grandfather can give to his grandson is time—time to share a walk, time to help him bait a hook, time to freely share confidences, time to teach his grandson how to pound in a nail, time to listen. Where distances or finances make regular interaction of this type difficult, the relationship between grandfather and grandson can be encouraged through phone calls and letters.

It means so much when a grandfather consistently and purposefully maintains a deep emotional and spiritual relationship with his grandson throughout his childhood, teenage years and adulthood. A grandfather can influence a growing boy in ways that a father cannot. A young man will often take advice from his grandfather that he would not even consider if it came from his father. In today's world, when one in two marriages end in divorce, the stability of a relationship with a grandfather does much to comfort and strengthen a boy or young man whose life is in turmoil.

Uncles Can Make a Difference

Grandfathers are not the only family members who play a vital role in guiding boys into manhood. Uncles provide their own brand of nurturing. They have the advantage of being one step removed from the immediate family, yet still very close to it. They are both close enough and distant enough to trust.

As I was growing up, my mother's brother often took time out for me. Sometimes he would come to my basketball games. When he entered the service, he'd write letters to me just to see how I was doing, and I would write back to him. It never seemed to matter to him what I was up to or how crazy I was; he was always accepting of me and willing to listen. His faithful acceptance and loving concern made it possible for me to accept constructive criticism from him that I would have rejected from other older men. Even today, although we live in different parts of the country, we are still able to talk about anything. It means so much to me to be able to share with him my thoughts and struggles about making a living and being a father, and to hear how he has struggled with some of the same things.

I was also privileged to have known my great-uncle, Bill Henslin, whom I spoke of in a previous chapter. He had already turned his farm over to his sons by the time I was a teenager and always seemed to have time to talk. A tall, gentle man, he entered politics when he was in his late sixties and served several terms as mayor of Dodge Center, Minnesota. I remember how he would talk with everyone we met as we walked around town together. A warm handshake, a caring smile, and often a mischievous wink communicated his sincere, deep interest in what was important to the people he encountered. In some ways, he was like a father to the whole community.

Bill's life was filled with rich relationships. Everyone had an almost immediate admiration and respect for him. His interest in his adult children, grandchildren, great-grandchildren, nephews, nieces, cousins, grand-nephews, and grand-nieces never waned. He was active and involved in his family and community until the day he died. Just by being around him and talking with him, boys, young men, and grown men soaked up the values, attitudes, and feelings that are crucial to living life.

Sadly, most young men today do not know what it is like to have a significant relationship with an uncle. Many men I have counseled do not even know the names of their uncles, and few uncles realize the positive impact they can have on their nephews' lives. Uncles have no idea how much a card or phone call can mean, or how to build the kind of relationship with their nephews that will help them grow into manhood.

Men Outside the Family Can Nurture a Boy's Maturity

All men who are close to a boy's family have a potential role to play in nurturing his masculine development, but this rarely happens these days. The men's community today, both in the church and in society-at-large, is underdeveloped. As a result, boys seldom have the support of other men as they attempt to make the necessary emotional break with their mothers. It is also rare for individual men to make the personal commitment necessary to nurture young boys. It is a tremendous blessing when an older man outside the family takes an interest in a boy.

Albert, who lived across the road from my parents' home for as long as I can remember, was someone who did this for me when I was a child. When I was only five or six years old, I would walk down the driveway and across the road to talk with Albert. No matter what he was doing, Albert had time for me. Sometimes he would stop his work and sit and talk; other times he would let me follow him around as he continued his chores.

As I grew older, I continued walking down the driveway to see Albert. During my confusing and bewildering teenage years, it meant a great deal to be able to enter the kitchen of Albert and Ann's house and feel accepted. During my busy college years, I continued to visit Albert whenever I came home.

It felt good just to talk with him. He showed his interest in me by asking what I was majoring in and what activities I enjoyed.

When Karen and I had our first child, I felt it was important to take the baby over to meet Albert. As Ben became older, he accompanied me on some of my visits with Albert because I wanted my son to have a relationship with a warm, caring, older man. In time, Ben began to visit with Albert on his own.

Albert generously gave to those who were younger than himself. He lived a simple life in a small, white clapboard house. He worked hard in his garden even though he had chronic arthritis in his knees and hips. He drove an old Chevy, but Albert also had four snowmobiles. He and his grandchildren liked snowmobiling and he kept all of those vehicles around just so he and his grandchildren could go snowmobiling together.

Several summers ago, when Albert and Ann were well into their eighties, Albert gave me a precious gift, a gift he may not have even realized he gave. He enabled me to see what a marriage commitment meant at the other end of life. I had gone over to his home early in the morning and found him working in the garden. We had talked for some time when he asked me if I wanted to see Ann before I went home. "She won't remember your name," he explained. "She may confuse you with your brother. Even if she does remember your name, she may ask you who you are a few minutes later. But don't worry about it. It's just the way things are now."

Albert's solid commitment to love and care for his wife through good times and bad, through sickness and health, deeply impressed me. Even though he suffered physically, he cared for Ann at home until he could do it no longer. He was deeply grieved when he finally had to put her into a nursing home, where she died a few months later. His faithful, caring commitment was a strong testimony to me of how much he loved Ann and what marriage meant.

After Albert died, which was on the day of his wedding anniversary, I learned that many men from the community had frequently stopped in to visit with him. Albert did not touch just my son, my brother, my brother's son, and me. He touched a whole community of men, from young boys to men in their sixties. Men stopped in to see him because Albert had a way of making a man feel loved and cared for, no matter who he was or how old he was. Men today need much more of this nurturing from an older man.

Every Man Needs A Friend

Most men have not had a close friend since they were teenagers or in their early twenties. By the time most men reach their mid-twenties, their career development and family concerns occupy first place in their lives. There is little time left for developing or deepening their relationships with other men. Men, however, need other men to surround them and support them as they go through life. Relationships with other men enable a man to deal with reality, to stay focused on what is important, and to put his life's energies into what is truly valuable.

When I suggest to the men I counsel that they need the support and closeness of other men, they often look at me in shock and disbelief. The idea of having an intimate, emotional and spiritual relationship with another man is beyond their comprehension. The main reason men do not consider close, supportive relationships with other men is, again, because of their father-son wound. Yet when men become aware of this wound and feel their loss deeply, they can begin to view other men as allies and resources for greater personal growth. They realize that good friends are crucial for masculine growth.

CHAPTER 8
▲▲▲▲▲▲▲▲▲▲▲

Building Bridges of Healing Between Father and Son

Several years ago, my father asked if he could attend a seminar that I was leading on the father-son wound. I was a bit surprised by his interest, but was happy that he wanted to come along. As the seminar began, I explained that I wanted to honor three special men in the group whom I would introduce one by one.

The first was Will Hawkins, M.D., my seminar co-leader. Will has been a close, supportive friend through more than ten years of good and painful times. Compassionate and caring, he not only has been used by God to heal people physically but has touched them spiritually as well.

The second was Bob Bartosh who, with his wife Pauline, founded Overcomers Outreach. An Alcoholics Anonymous member with eighteen years of sobriety, Bob has modeled Christ's love and acceptance by sticking with me through all kinds of situations.

The third man I introduced was my father.

All three men are in their sixties and each has been a kind of father to me. God has used them to touch my emotions and spirit deeply. One man is my birth father. One man is an emotional father who has been a solid mentor in my business and profession, holding me and praying with me through difficult times. And one man has been a fatherly role model, demonstrating through his own life an honest, twelve-step recovery program.

As I introduced these men, a deep sobbing came over me. I was overpowered by a grief that sent tears rolling down my cheeks. I was overwhelmed by a feeling of loss in my relationship with my father. Here he was in the same room with two men with whom I have the type of relationship I desired to have with him.

I looked up for a moment and saw tears in my father's eyes—tears that came from his own deep sadness and emptiness in his relationship with his own father, and tears that flowed for me and the sadness I carried. At that moment it did not matter to me that I cried in the presence of nearly one hundred men I had never met before. What mattered was that God had given me a deep and precious gift, the chance to see my father shed tears for me.

Fathers Are Wounded Too

My father's acknowledgment and expression of pain in that meeting was necessary for my healing and for his. Healing will not occur between father and son unless the father is willing to face his own woundedness, which for most men is a foreign concept. Healing between father and son requires the son to recognize and accept his father's woundedness, which can only occur after the son has experienced some healing as well.

It is so important to remember that the little boy within all men desires affirmation, approval, and acceptance. Although we can each say to ourselves, *I've done a great job,* we long to hear that praise from men who are important to us. Nothing beats hearing our fathers say, "Son, I'm proud of you."

Like most men, I knew my father cared about me but never heard him express those feelings directly. Consequently, I felt frustrated and hurt in my relationship with him. I also felt ashamed for having those feelings. After all, I knew in my head that my father loved me, but I could not feel it in my gut. That gut-level experience was necessary for me, just as it is in the life of every boy and every man.

When it dawned on me that my father did not know how to express his love for me because he had never experienced such love from his father, I began to recognize that the little boy within him was as wounded as the one within me. My grandfather had been unable to directly express that he loved my father and valued him as his son. In fact, many of my grandfather's actions showed favor to my father's brother and rejection of my father. My grandfather's actions communicated that my father was inadequate, that he could not be entrusted with responsibility, and that he was unworthy to be blessed with reward. The final, crushing blow came when my grandfather died and left the entire estate to my father's older brother. My father's brother confirmed the message of my father's unworthiness by accepting the entire estate, sharing none of it with his brother. Their combined actions conveyed a terrible, shaming message to my father, who for years had worked side by side with his father and older brother. The whole scenario deeply wounded my father, as it would any man.

Although I am proud of many things in my family, this story is not pretty. If healing is to occur, the dark side of that woundedness must be recognized and accepted for what it is. My father has begun to recognize his woundedness. He is beginning to recognize how his father's lack of positive expression of love hurt him deeply as he was growing up. As a result, he is trying to more openly express his feelings toward family members. He is beginning to tell us how he feels rather than assuming that we will already know how he feels by his actions.

As we learned in the previous chapter, the key to healing the father-son wound is for men to begin to experience their own feelings, to bring out the deep wound within them, and to learn to share the pain of that wound with other men. When men do this, the stage is set for them to develop relationships on a much deeper level. As part of my own recovery, I had to go through stages of grief and anger about what I had not received, and probably would never receive, in my relationship with my father. Through the process of dealing with my own woundedness, I began to see my father's woundedness and accept him for who he is. This acceptance is a necessary step in building strong emotional bridges between fathers and sons.

Like Father, Like Son

I would like to share an unusual story with you. It is about a father and son who each took the painful risk of delving into their feelings. It shows how the father-son wound affects a family for generations. It also shows what can happen when an adult son and his father choose to deal with that wound and work toward healing in their relationship.

Doug had worked hard to provide well for his family. When he was a child, his father, an alcoholic, had only worked during his brief periods of sobriety. Doug hated the shame of growing up on the wrong side of the tracks. His shame was magnified because his family lived in a small town where everyone knew about everyone else. When he became a teenager, Doug vowed that his children would never suffer the way he had.

Doug kept his vow. His family did not suffer because of a lack of material things, but they suffered deeply nonetheless. Doug traveled extensively for his job and even when he was home, work was still his first priority. It seemed as if he always had a pile of paperwork to complete that kept him from spending time with his son, John. Although he never said much about it, John deeply missed his father's time and attention. In fact when he was a teenager, John bitterly vowed that he would never work the long hours his father worked.

Like his father, John kept his vow. He was home by 4:30 every afternoon. He never missed a school conference. He attended every ball game, was present for every camping trip, and took part in every special program. But something was not quite right in John's life. He came to me for counseling because of deep depression. Although fully involved in his children's activities, he seemed unable to connect with them on a deeper emotional and spiritual level. John did not realize it at first, but he responded to his children with the same emotional coolness he had experienced in his relationship with his father. Since he had not experienced an emotional connection with his father, he did not know how to connect with his children.

As John progressed in counseling, he connected with the grief he bore as a result of never feeling close to his father. Through many tears, he grieved over the loss of his relationship with his father. As he faced his grief, he was able to relate to his children on an emotional and spiritual as well as on a physical level. In time John realized that his relationship with his father was the primary issue he needed to resolve, so he asked his father to join him in counseling. Through our counseling sessions, Doug began to share his feelings about John's lifestyle. He did not feel that John was working hard enough for his family or that John would have enough money to send his children to college. He wished that John lived in a more expensive neighborhood. He even hated the old car John drove!

Can you see what was happening? John had chosen a different lifestyle than his father had chosen. He provided for his family, but did not accumulate wealth. In a pattern typical of the grandchild of an alcoholic, John had chosen to grow in the experience and expression of his feelings. His greatest desire was to be a family man, a husband and father who was deeply involved with his wife and children. The choices John had made triggered many of his father's unresolved issues.

In subsequent sessions Doug began to feel the pain of what he had missed in his relationship with his father. He discovered within himself a shamed little boy who had been embarrassed by his father's alcoholism and negligence in providing for his family. He also grieved over what he had lost in his relationship with his son. He realized he had been somewhat jealous of the time John spent with his family and felt shamed because he had not spent more time with John when he was younger. Without realizing it, Doug had refused to face those feelings in himself. Instead, he had been directing the anger and sadness he felt in his relationship with his father toward his son.

It was a special moment when Doug felt the sadness of his son's loss and John felt a deep compassion for his father's woundedness. Each man shed tears for the other. By feeling each other's pain, father and son experienced an emotional bond that they had never known before. John became free to honor his father for providing for his family, and Doug gained a new respect for his son. He was set free to recognize John's need to live out the values that were important to him. This freedom and growth in intimacy would never have taken place if Doug and John had not taken the risk of experiencing the grief of their father-son wound.

An Adult Son Needs an Emotional Bridge to His Father

If men are to be fully men, an emotional bridge between father and son must exist. Doug and John made tremendous strides in their masculine growth when they worked through their respective father-son wounds and established an emotional bond. Their newly discovered intimacy enabled them to gain a respect, admiration and acceptance of one another that they had never experienced before.

Every man would benefit from an emotionally intimate relationship with his father. Every man has a deep longing to be honored, respected and admired by an older man. If a man has a father who can give of himself emotionally, God has given him a great gift. Unfortunately, few men today have received this gift, so it is important that men seek out older men who can play an active role in their lives.

Robert Moore, a psychologist who has done extensive writing and speaking on men's issues and the full scope of masculine development, has said that a man is wounded if he is not admired by an older man at least once a week.[1] I could not agree with him more. Simply by being a part of my life, Will Hawkins, Bob Bartosh, and Bill Henslin have admired me, and that high regard has helped heal my woundedness. I look up to these men and see something in each of their lives that helps me grow a bit more. When these men compliment me or respond to me, they touch the wounded little boy within. When I listen to their words, my soul becomes a little richer. In turn, my listening shows them honor and respect and reminds them that their struggles in life have been worthwhile.

If you are the father of an adult son, you can be sure that he has a deep desire to hear you say that you love him. He wants to know without a doubt that you approve of the man he is. If you are not giving your adult son that affirmation on a continual basis, his woundedness will continue to grow. It is never too late to begin this process. No matter how old your son is, you can move toward healing in your relationship with him and begin to offer him the affirmation and approval he needs.

A Father Needs Support for Building a Bridge to His Son

It is normal for a father, once he has become aware of his woundedness in his relationship with his father and has connected with his deep grief, to feel great sadness for the loss his son has suffered. The father's own grief prompts him to want to move toward a more feeling relationship with his son, to build an emotional bridge to him. Many fathers are relieved to know that no matter how long the emotional bridge between father and son has been broken, it is never too late for a father to take steps to build that bridge.

A father must realize, however, that building an emotional bridge to an adult son is no easy task. This process carries significant emotional risk for both father and son. To handle those emotional risks, it is tremendously important that a father be well established in his own recovery and have a strong support group for himself before he reaches out to his adult son.

One reason support is necessary is that many fathers feel a great amount of guilt and shame when they realize how they have wounded their sons. At times this guilt is so great that a father will stop making progress in his own healing. But if he has the support of other men, they can help him focus on his continued growth and help him learn to forgive himself for what has happened.

The whole idea of forgiving oneself is very important. On his own, a man cannot father a son on a deeper emotional level than he experienced from his father. A man has to give himself a great deal of grace as he seeks to build an emotional bond with his adult son. He has to realize that he, just like every other man in the world, is learning how to be a father. The support of other men is invaluable to him as he grows into new levels of fatherhood.

A father also needs to give up the notion that he can father perfectly. It simply cannot be done. Only God can father perfectly. A father needs to accept the reality that his best efforts will not fully meet his son's needs. Some fathers, for example, must spend significant time away from home and their children in order to do their jobs. Even when a father is home, he cannot meet every emotional need. I have four children. I can only be emotionally available to one child at a time, which means I'm unavailable to the other three at any given moment. It is easier to accept my limitations as a father when I have the perspective and support of close relationships with other men.

I encourage fathers to also remember that it has only recently become acceptable for men to recognize and express their feelings. Emotional awareness is a new experience for many men, particularly those who grew up in the thirties and forties. Until just a few years ago, both the Christian community and secular culture considered the reality of masculine emotion to be unimportant. Even principles put forth in most Christian parenting books basically ignored the child's and the parent's feelings. Since such a fundamental aspect of father-son relationships has been ignored, it is no wonder that a great emotional gap exists between most fathers and their sons.

The active support of other men can do much to help a father understand, sort out, and learn to express the feeling side of his masculinity. It can help prepare him to take steps toward healing in his relationship with his adult son. It can also help him handle the ups and downs of his son's responses as he tries to move closer to him.

If a son meets his father's emotional overtures with an angry, resentful, or silent response, support for the father is essential. A man is hurt when he does not receive the response he desires from his son. When a father is hurt in this way, it is all too easy for him to relapse into anger, shame and rejection of his son. If a father has the support of other men, however, he can express his frustration and hurt to them. His support group can encourage him and pray with him that God will open a door in his son's heart. They can help the father bear the pain of trying to build an emotional bridge to his son.

Building a Bridge from Father to Son

After honestly evaluating their existing relationship, a father must take his first steps toward his adult son with great care. Some fathers have a pretty good relationship with their adult sons, so a move toward emotional intimacy deepens and enriches what they already enjoy. Other fathers have never been close to their adult sons, so their overtures may be greeted with suspicion or resentment. They will have a more difficult time establishing an emotional bond with their sons. Some fathers have been physically or emotionally abusive, so their sons may respond to any contact with distrust and rage. These men face a long and difficult road when they seek healing in their relationships with their adult sons.

A father must never forget that he cannot control the process of healing in his relationship with his son. Healing of the father-son relationship will not occur unless the son is open to it. The longer the emotional bridge between father and son has been down, the greater the son's anger, suspicion and resentment toward his father. It is not unusual for a son, particularly if he is living in denial or under the influence of addictions, to reject his father's attempts at establishing an emotional relationship. That is why it is important that a father who wants to take positive steps toward reconnecting with his son set good boundaries. A father who seeks to build an emotional bond with his son cannot afford to take his son's initial reaction personally, nor can he afford to be defensive. Both of these common responses are destructive to the healing process.

A father who seeks a deeper emotional relationship with his son can offer no excuses for what has happened in the past. Excuses mean nothing to an adult son who has been hurt. A father simply needs to take responsibility for the ways in which he has wounded his son, express his deep sorrow for having done so, and hang in there while his son works through what-ever emotions the father's approach has unleashed.

When a father has been uninvolved in his son's life for a long time, the son may respond to his efforts with frustration, defensiveness or denial. The reason for this is clear. Inside the adult son is a little boy who is waiting to see if the involvement his father now promises will really come to pass. While the son was growing up, there might have been periods when his father was close to him—until the next promotion came along and the father started working long hours again.

A father cannot expect years of woundedness to be brushed aside just because he now wants to make amends. A father must give his son time to work through his anger and sadness about the loss in their relationship. A son needs time to learn how to trust again. It may take a month, six months, or even longer for the son to work through his grief, anger, and lack of trust in his father. Waiting through this process is never easy, but a father must remember that dealing with the anger is part of the process, and that the anger will not last forever. The son simply needs a season of time to grow and heal.

Waiting for a son to work through his emotions regarding his father is particularly hard for Christian fathers. As Christians, we tend to think that if we apologize, others should immediately forgive us and everything should be wonderful. The truth is, nothing in Christianity equates human forgiveness with trust. Forgiveness and trust are separate issues. Forgiveness is a one-time action a person chooses to make; trust is a cumulative result of experiences over time.

Therefore it is vitally important that a father remain emotionally available to a son who is working through loss and grief. If a son greets his father's movement toward him with distrust and anger, it is easy for a father to back off and close the door to further intimacy. Yet if a father is far enough along in his own recovery and has the support of other men, he can remain emotionally close to his son during this difficult time. A father can listen as his son expresses the deep emotions he feels regarding their relationship. He can acknowledge and accept responsibility for the ways in which he has hurt his son and also establish firm boundaries within himself so that he does not accept blame for wrongs he has not committed.

One reason boundaries are important is because a son may become abusive as his father moves toward him emotionally. A father must not allow himself to become a victim of his son's anger. He may need to say to his son, "I'm here to talk with you about your anger and hurt. I want to listen to you, but I won't allow you to yell at me or abuse me."

In this type of situation, support is crucial. A father may need to find a third person, such as a pastor or therapist, who is knowledgeable about these issues and is willing to be involved in the reconciliation process. More and more frequently I receive calls from parents who say, "We're really distant from our adult children and would like to begin rebuilding those relationships at a deeper level. Can you help us do that?" There is nothing wrong or shameful about seeking the help of others in the healing process because both father and son are covering much new ground as they reconnect emotionally.

A father may need the help of a third person if his son has been sexually abused by himself or others. The wound of sexual abuse seems to go deeper into a man's soul than all other wounds. It destroys a man's trust in other men. A son who has suffered sexual abuse may be extremely resistant to establishing emotional intimacy with his father. This is true even when someone other than the father was the abuser. Furthermore, a son who has been sexually abused may be not be consistent in his relationship with his father. The father may think their relationship is going well when all of a sudden his son will withdraw or become angry. A father must not take his son's inconsistent response personally because this response may stem from the wound of sexual abuse and not the wound of the father-son relationship. All fathers need to be aware of this possibility and have a strong support system available so they can deal with it.

I cannot emphasize enough how important it is for a father to have the steadfast support of other men as he takes steps toward greater emotional intimacy with his adult son. A father who can share with other men his feelings about drawing close to his son will have stronger boundaries. If a father takes these steps on his own, without any support, he may be devastated by his son's response and withdraw or revert back to old ways of relating to his son.

Practical Steps for Building Bridges

When a father makes an effort to bridge the emotional gap between himself and his adult son, he is taking a tremendous step. When he realizes the impact of his previous actions upon his son's life, he may wonder where to start. There is no "right place" to begin. A father can take steps toward emotional intimacy with his son in a number of different ways, depending on the kind of relationship he already has with his son and the physical distance between them.

One father and son began by attending a men's conference together. This made it easier for them to begin talking about the deep issues between them, issues that had been too awkward to discuss before. Recently the father, who is retiring, called his son and said, "You know, since the sale of the business has gone through, I'll have time to do some things. I know you're busy, but I'd really like to go skiing with you. We haven't done that since you were a teenager! If there's any way you can get away for a few days, I'll pay the airfare. Let's do it!" That man's son was thrilled. He responded just like an enthusiastic little kid. He rearranged his work schedule so he could go, and the two of them had a great time together.

Most adult sons are not used to their fathers initiating joint activities. It makes a tremendous impact when the father says, "Let's go camping. Let's do something together—just you and me—so we can have a chance to get to know each other better." Fathers should be aware, however, that some sons may show no interest in the activities their fathers initiate. In that situation the father must accept his son's choice, but he should not give up. He should wait for a while and then extend another invitation. The son may be waiting to see if his father will really follow through on what he says he wants to do.

For some fathers and sons, a weekend together would be too much time to spend with each other, at least at first. If that is the case, a father can invite his son out for lunch. I know one adult son who never misses a lunch with his dad. The father listens to his son and then prays with him about what he is going through. The son benefits by not only knowing that his father wants to spend time with him, but also by receiving the deep blessing of his father praying for him.

If physical distance between a father and his son is a problem, phone calls and letters can do much to open up a deeper relationship between them. A father does not need to write and call to the extent that he bothers his son, but he can express interest in how his son is doing and what is happening in his life. When a father initiates this type of communication, it may pave the way for spending more time with his son.

All of these steps can help establish an emotional relationship through which a father and son can begin to address their deeper issues. When the time is right, the father can initiate a discussion with his son about the times he knows he has wounded him. He can express sorrow about hurting his son and can clearly take responsibility for making amends. From that point on, the son's response determines the father's next step toward emotional intimacy. If the son responds to his father with an openness to further sharing, the emotional bridge is beginning to be established.

Building a Bridge from Son to Father

Every young son *needs* his father to reach out and establish an emotional bond with him. This is not something a child can do for himself; his father must do it for him. Many fathers have not done this, nor do they have a clue that an emotional bridge between father and son can or needs to exist. Some adult sons, however, have become aware of their need for an emotional bond with their fathers and want to make that happen. Often these adult sons have already come face to face with their father-son wound through their efforts to overcome addictions or to live on a deeper emotional level. In the depths of their souls, they have felt the loss of a relationship with their fathers and desire to develop an emotional bond with them.

I assure adult sons that it is possible, but not ideal, for them to initiate the risky first steps toward establishing an emotional relationship with their fathers. I urge sons who want to do this to use great caution. We have already seen how risky this reaching out can be for the father of an adult son, and it is an even riskier step for the son to take.

It is essential that the adult son be in a strong recovery program before he attempts to reach out to his father. This means that the son must deal deeply with the grief of his father-son wound. He must develop solid, emotional relationships with other men and learn how to deal with the painful memories of his relationship with his father through their support. He must learn how to set boundaries in his relationships so that he does not fall into old, harmful patterns of relating to others.

A strong, ongoing recovery program and adequate support are particularly important if a man's father is in denial and does not understand the significance or depth of the father-son wound. A father who is in denial will probably not give his adult son the emotional response the son seeks. This can be devastating to a man who is reaching out. A shaming or controlling response can prompt a son who lacks adequate support to relapse into his addictions. If a father already has some openness in his relationship with his son, there is less chance that his response will be so devastating.

An adult son who wants to establish an emotional bond with his father would also be well advised to respect the positive benefits his father has tried to provide through the years and to recognize his father's predicament. Most fathers faithfully provided for their sons' material needs and had no idea that their sons required anything more. Some fathers sacrificed greatly, denying their own needs, in order to provide for their families. My own father has lived through years of pain from arthritic knees and a deteriorating back, both results of the hard physical labor he performed on the farm. I need to feel the value of the sacrifice he made for me. Although recognizing the father's past sacrifices does not take away a son's pain, it is important that at some point the son be able to value the good his father has given to him.

An adult son must never forget that his father also bears a deep wound in his relationship with his own father. He must recognize that his father's wound has greatly influenced how he relates to his son. A son may go through a time of grieving for his father when he recognizes that a wounded little boy also resides within his father. If the father has suffered sexual abuse, the son may need to accept the fact that his father has been so deeply wounded that he will never be the father the son would like him to be.

Very few fathers have had the opportunity to discover the feeling side of their masculinity or to recognize their own woundedness. Men as a whole are just beginning to discover what a feeling masculinity is all about. Most fathers need to be educated about these issues. They may have no idea what recovery is all about. In the minds of many fathers, recovery is something that happens to the economy, not to people. To them, recovery is what you do after you have bypass surgery.

I take this need for education into account when I counsel a father and son together. I explain that this is an opportunity for both of them to learn something new. I assure the father that he cannot be expected to know how to do something he has never experienced himself. A father is usually responsive when approached this way. I can then talk about the grief in the hearts of men—grief that comes from not being blessed by one's father, from being shamed by one's father, and so on. When I begin sharing stories of the grief in men's hearts, it is rare for a father not to connect with his own inner pain. Often the door is open for father and son to do some deep sharing and crying together. When they connect with each other's grief, their relationship is forever changed.

Change Doesn't Mean Perfection

It is a special moment when a father and son share some of their grief together and begin to build the emotional bridge between them. This does not mean, however, that all is now well in their relationship. If a father and son sincerely desire to continue building their relationship, they have a great deal of work to do. Both must deal with the old hurts and new challenges of their life together. This is not an easy thing to do, so they must proceed with patience and deep commitment.

A father and son who want to strengthen their emotional bond must not expect perfection. Both of them will make mistakes that will hurt the other. This kind of hurt is difficult to deal with when the relationship has been strained and stretched. When a misunderstanding arises, or when the father or son relapse into old ways of relating to each other, it is all too easy to assume that nothing in their relationship has really changed or ever will. In these situations, the father and son need to remember that God alone is perfect and unfailing. They need to remind themselves that, yes, some things in their relationship have changed and that other changes will occur if they continue to work at it. A father and son must be patient as they rebuild their trust in one another.

Rebuilding trust means that they must agree to deal with the old hurts that undermine their relationship. A man does not fully trust a man who has hurt him in the past, so healing of these old wounds must take place before the new father-son relationship can grow. Healing takes place when a father or son can share openly about deep hurts and resentments and know that the other man wants to hear him and respond to his pain. One adult son told his father how humiliated he had felt as a teenager when his father had teased him. His father did not become defensive, but acknowledged how he had hurt his son without intending to do so. He then told his son he was sorry and promised that he would work on not shaming him again. This type of sharing strengthens the emotional bridge.

Healing between father and son will not occur if old, hurtful feelings are ignored or pushed away. A father and son must learn how to express their feelings directly. Most men make mistakes as they learn this new skill, so they must be patient with one another. When a father and son can safely bring the pain of past wounds out into the open and respond to this pain with genuine sorrow and forgiveness, the emotional bridge between them grows much stronger.

However, no father-son relationships are perfect, so a father and son may hurt each other as their relationship deepens. It is important that fathers and sons trust one another enough to directly express their feelings about current wounds as well as old ones. When I turned forty years old, every member of my family congratulated me except my father. I was already saddened by the fact I was leaving a decade of my life behind, and my father's apparent lack of interest greatly burdened me. After two weeks had passed without a word from him, I wrote to my father and told him that I had been hurt because he had not called me or sent me a card. When my father received my letter, he called me right away. With tears in his voice, he said he was sorry that he had hurt me. We talked about my sadness and about his sadness as well. As we connected with our feelings, the anger and resentment I had been feeling toward him lifted. It was not easy for us to talk about these feelings, but we have agreed to do so because it is the only way we can continue growing in our relationship.

Strengthening the bond between fathers and sons is not all work. Fathers and sons who want to continue building their relationship need to take some time for what my son and I call "men's stuff." Men's stuff is whatever a father and son do when they take the time to enjoy an experience together. For some fathers and sons, this may be an all-day fishing trip. For others, it may be a backpacking or whitewater rafting trip. For still other fathers and sons, it may be sharing a meal together and going to their favorite baseball team's opening game. For my son Ben and me, men's stuff is the Rosarito-Ensenada bike ride.

Ben and I have taken this fifty-mile bike ride together every year for the past five years. We even went, via tandem bicycle, the year Ben broke his arm a few days before the ride. The route winds along Mexico's Pacific coast, then climbs from sea level to twelve hundred feet in a grueling, eight-mile stretch of switchbacks. When I'm pedaling up that stretch, I always wonder why I do it, but I wouldn't trade anything for the exhilaration of standing at the top with my arm around Ben and basking in our conquest. After the ride we head for the beaches and cliffs where we play and relax until nightfall. Then we shoot off the fireworks we've picked up along the way. This kind of men's stuff is very good for strengthening the bond between father and son.

Bridge-Building for a Lifetime

The father who really has an advantage in building an emotional bridge between father and son is the one who becomes aware of his own woundedness while his children are still young—even before they are born. This father has the opportunity to think about what he wants in his relationship with his son. He can make the choices that help ensure a close relationship from infancy through adulthood. He can take the daily steps in the healing of his own father-son wound that will enable him to build a bond with his son.

A father who has plunged into the reality of his own pain will feel more deeply what it means to be a father and will be much more sensitive to his son's feelings. A father who is emotionally connected with other men on whom he can depend for mentoring and support as he grows into fatherhood—men with whom he can share his worries, fears, and dreams about being a father—will find it easier to be emotionally close to his son. A father who is emotionally close to another man whose fathering he admires has a valuable resource for dealing with the practical, day-to-day problems of fathering. The son of such a man will be fortunate indeed.

As the son grows, he will have a father who knows how good a loving hug at the right time feels, even to a teenager. He will be able to talk to his father about almost anything. He will have a father who sincerely cares about things that are important to him, whether it be competitive sports, playing the piano or collecting comic books. He will have a father who makes promises his son can count on. A father who deals with his woundedness has the hope of passing on these, and many more gifts to his son.

No matter what stage of fatherhood a man is in, no matter what his age, it is helpful for him to realize the magnitude of what he is doing when he takes steps to build an emotional bridge between generations. His efforts may represent the first time in generations that any healing interaction has taken place in the family. Such a step is truly historic. It may be the first time two generations of his family have connected on a deep emotional level.

When a man takes such a step and sticks with it, his decision will have a positive impact upon his family for generations to come. Building emotional bridges requires tremendous courage and occurs only after a man has passed through the painful process of facing his own woundedness. But the man's children, grandchildren and even great-grandchildren will feel the rewards of such an effort. Such a man leaves a legacy that will be felt for many years to come.

CHAPTER **9**
▲▲▲▲▲▲▲▲▲▲▲

N urturing Masculine Growth for a Lifetime

When a man begins to deal with the pain and issues related to his damaged relationship with his father, he has a greatly increased capacity to develop his masculine potential. Masculine growth entails much more than achieving a degree of healing in one's relationship with one's father. Masculine growth entails the full development of all aspects of a man's being—including his spirit, emotions, talents, and accomplishments. It entails the development of a man's potential at every stage of life—his potential to be an intimate husband, a loving father, a spiritual leader, a master in his chosen vocation and a wise and generous old man.

Masculine growth is an intimidating process. The good news is that it is not supposed to happen overnight, does not happen as the result of one event, and is never complete. It is intended to be a lifelong process. Most important, *it is a process that must be nurtured through relationships with other men.* The process of men encouraging and nurturing masculine development in other men is called *initiation.*

126

Initiation Isn't What You Think It Is

To most American men, the word *initiation* conjures up images of Boy Scout ceremonies, secret rituals between pre-adolescent friends, or bizarre fraternity hazings. None of these images represent the kind of lifelong nurturing that fuels masculine growth. The whole concept of initiation is, for the most part, unknown in our culture today. The type of initiation that fosters and supports masculine development, however, can still be found in the practices of various tribal societies.

Within the aboriginal societies that practice male initiation, there comes a time in a boy's life when the older men physically take him away from his mother and bring him into the world of men. The men of the tribe make a symbolic and physical break between the boy and his mother. He usually does not see her for an extended period of time and, following his initiation, he will never live with her again. The boy's initiation is often an intense training time during which his physical, emotional, and spiritual skills are greatly expanded and tempered. He may have to accomplish difficult tasks, be required to go through a time of fasting, and have to endure pain—all in the company of the men of his tribe. These activities take place within the context of ritualistic ceremonies in which the whole company of men participates. These ceremonies involve the telling of legends that communicate the history of the tribe and perhaps song, dance or poetry that portrays the heroics of previous generations. Depending on the tribe, the initiation process may take several years to complete.

It is not difficult to see how such a process would cause a boy to feel as if he belongs in the world of men. This type of experience would instill the values, history and traditions of male society into the boy's very being. It would teach a boy that the men of his community were a valuable resource to him. Assessing the function of primitive tribal rituals, Ray Raphael describes what initiation accomplishes:

The most important and sweeping function of a primitive initiation was to provide a youth with a sense of his own personal significance within the context of a greater world. In becoming a man he took his place alongside his father and forefathers; by discovering his tribal heritage he became connected with the ongoing flow of life. He was transformed into a spiritual being as he joined his ancestors in a universal brotherhood that cut through time.[1]

Robert Bly also interprets the significant message of initiation for men today: "The ancient societies believed that a boy becomes a man only through ritual and effort—that he must be initiated into the world of men. It does not happen by itself, it does not happen just because he eats Wheaties. And only men can do this work."[2]

One tragedy of American culture today is that the process of initiation, the intentional process of causing boys to become men, has been basically abandoned. Fathers and older men no longer nurture boys into manhood. Instead, boys are left to their own devices, and the results are devastating. In the introduction of *To Be a Man*, Keith Thompson recognizes these harmful results and offers the following analysis of our present situation:

When a culture ceases to provide specific, meaningful initiatory pathways, the individual male psyche is left to initiate itself. And therein lies a great danger, visible in the kinds of initiation to which many men turn: street gangs, drug and alcohol abuse, high-risk sports, militarism, discipleship to charismatic cult leaders, obsessive workplace competition, compulsive relocation of home and job, serial sexual conquests, pursuit of the "perfect" (and thus unattainable) older male mentor, and so forth.[3]

In the same book, Robert Moore and Douglas Gillette comment on the personal pain some men suffer because of this missing element in male development:

A man who "cannot get it together" is a man who has probably not had the opportunity to undergo ritual initiation into the deep structures of manhood. He remains a boy—not because he wants to, but because no one has shown him the way to transform his boy energies into man energies. No one has led him into direct and healing experiences of the inner world of the masculine potentials.[4]

For most men, masculine potential remains a mystery. The impact of a solid community of physically, emotionally and spiritually developed men on our society remains unknown. Initiation has been absent from our culture for so long that men do not even know what it is. And all of us—men, women, children—suffer from its absence.

The Need for Initiation Today

As families, as a Christian community, and as a society, we do little to recognize the stages of a man's development and even less to nurture his growth through those stages. What little initiation we do have is at best superficial. Consider the following common milestones of a young man's growth in society today:

- It is a big step when a young man gets a driver's license, yet a driver's license provides little more than legal access to an expensive, lethal weapon.
- Many young men (and the older men they admire) consider themselves to have arrived at a new threshold of manhood when they have sexual relations for the first time. For many, unfortunately, this occurs prior to marriage.
- Being part of a high school varsity team is an accomplishment many young boys anticipate. They look up to the juniors and seniors on the team and admire them as men. The boys feel that if they could one day be part

of that elite group, they would become more than boys. Although it is true that being on a team gives a young man a sense of belonging, that camaraderie often does little to nurture his growth on a deep emotional and spiritual level. In fact, much of what is shared hinders rather than fosters masculine maturity. For example, stories that are shared about sexual conquests are dehumanizing, whereas a true initiation process deepens a man's respect for women, God and other men.

• High school graduation is a true milestone, an opportunity to nurture a young man's maturity at a deep level. Although this passage is recognized through a formal ceremony, a deeper nurturing rarely takes place. Graduation often is little more than an excuse to attend an all-night party.

• A young man goes off to college and begins a new era of life. With the exception of contact with professors or coaches, most young men are at this point cut off from the nurturing influence of older men. In the absence of the older generation's influence, amidst peers who also need nurturing, a young man's life may take bizarre twists.

• Catechism and confirmation classes have some of the characteristics and potential of initiation. Yet for most young men, the potential of these experiences is lost. Why is this so? First, a young man often endures these classes only because his parents make him do it. Second, those who teach the classes are often unaware of the potential for deep growth and take a superficial approach to the process. Third, the community of men in the church may not model or actively support the principles and values that are taught through these classes.

• Perhaps the closest initiation experience a young man has today is his military training. Basic training is designed to be a growth-producing process. The instructor's job is to push his recruits hard, to see what they are made of, to see how much they can master, to see what they can endure physically and emotionally. When their training is over, the men usually go out and celebrate together. They have earned the right to become a part of all the men who are in military service. They have an undeniable bond with a whole group of men. Yet the experience and sense of belonging that has traditionally been a part of military service has diminished in the years since Vietnam; it does not produce as strong a bond as it once did.

It is not difficult to see how these forms of initiation fall short of what young men need, for they offer little impact on a deep emotional level. God created young men with a need to be trained and nurtured into their full masculine development, so the need for initiation is still very much a part of every young man's being. When initiation is absent, young men seek it out on their own.

Jay, for example, found his own initiation into manhood through his use of cocaine. As a teenager, he felt empowered when he used the drug. His feeling of importance was enhanced because he used cocaine with a group of older teenagers. By being accepted as part of their group, he felt as if he had a place in the world of men. Other uninitiated young men may turn to gangs, crime or the pursuit of sexual experiences as a way to achieve acceptance and status as men.

True initiation is not an option; it is a necessity. Not one of the false initiations described above comes close to accomplishing what young men need. One reason these experiences fall short is because there is a dire shortage of spiritually and emotionally alive men who recognize the need and are willing to take their place in nurturing masculine growth in younger men. As young men grow into manhood, they need the active involvement of older men who have wrestled, suffered and grown into their own masculine identity. Our society desperately needs what these older men have to offer.

Initiation Is an Important Function for the Christian Community

I believe the process of nurturing men is one that the community of Christian men needs to take seriously and in which it needs to become fully involved. For the most part, Christian men have not considered it their business or responsibility to nurture one another or to nurture young men, although they will readily acknowledge their spiritual need for discipleship. Initiation and discipleship, however, are not as different as we might think. It is entirely appropriate, and even necessary, for Christian men to actively nurture masculine development.

The Christian community of men can do much to help a young boy become a man, to guide him along his lifelong physical, spiritual and emotional journey. Christian men who are committed to God can help a young man go through the painful process of making an emotional break with his family and discovering an identity apart from his family. The strong support of a community of Christian men can help a young man mature into the spiritual and relational responsibilities of manhood. Christian men can do much to affirm, encourage and challenge one another as they discover and cultivate their spiritual gifts. When the time is right, a young man can take his place among his peers in the Christian community and begin initiating those younger than himself as he continues to be nurtured by the older men of the community.

In Scripture, we can find a number of illustrations of initiations that nurture a man's development. Let us consider the major elements of initiation that are evident in the lives of several well-known Bible characters.

Initiation Moves a Boy from the World of His Parents Into the World of Men

One of the first major steps a young man takes as he develops into manhood is to make an emotional break from his childhood—to emotionally separate himself from his mother and to step into the world of men. For many young men this is a difficult step. Samuel, however, was a very fortunate young man. He was born under unusual circumstances to parents who had a strong spiritual commitment. As a result of their commitment, his parents facilitated his entrance into the world of men. Let us take a closer look at his story.

Hannah, wife of Elkanah, had been barren for many years. One year, when Hannah and Elkanah were at Shiloh to offer their annual sacrifice to the Lord, Hannah prayed earnestly for a child:

> In bitterness of soul Hannah wept much and prayed to
> the Lord. And she made a vow, saying, "O Lord Almighty,
> if you will only look upon your servant's misery and remem-
> ber me, and not forget your servant but give her a son,
> then I will give him to the Lord for all the days of his life,
> and no razor will ever be used on his head."
>
> 1 Samuel 1:10–11

Eli, the priest, saw her praying and rebuked her because he thought she was drunk. When she explained that the fervent nature of her prayers was because of her sorrow that she had no child, he sent her on her way with the words, "Go in peace, and may the God of Israel grant you what you have asked of him" (1 Samuel 1:17). In due time Hannah gave birth to Samuel.

The first year after his birth, Hannah did not take Samuel to Shiloh when Elkanah went to make his yearly sacrifice to God. Although Elkanah was ready to fulfill his vow, he recognized that Hannah had to fulfill her commitment to God when she was ready. She asked him to let her wait until she had weaned Samuel. Notice his beautiful response to her request: "'Do what seems best to you,' Elkanah her husband told her. 'Stay here until you have weaned him; only may the Lord make good his word'" (1 Samuel 1:23).

Hannah kept her commitment. While Samuel was still a very young child, he was brought to the temple to begin training to fulfill his lifelong responsibilities. This turning point in Samuel's life was not made casually, but was marked by a significant ceremony.

> After he was weaned, she took the boy with her, young as he was, along with a three-year-old bull, an ephah of flour and a skin of wine, and brought him to the house of the Lord at Shiloh. When they had slaughtered the bull, they brought the boy to Eli, and she said to him, "As surely as you live, my lord, I am the woman who stood here beside you praying to the Lord. I prayed for this child, and the Lord has granted me what I asked of him. So now I give him to the Lord. For his whole life he will be given over to the Lord."
>
> 1 Samuel 1:24–28

It was no easy task for the family to travel to Shiloh, which probably took several days. It also wasn't easy to kill and sacrifice a three-year-old bull. It certainly was not easy for Hannah and Elkanah to let go of such a young child; yet the ceremony was appropriate in light of the significance of the break that was being made between Samuel and his family. Hannah and Elkanah were acutely aware that they were giving their son back to God. From that point on, Samuel would continue the process of training and development for God's service, with Eli as his mentor.

In Luke 2:41-52 we see an emotional break from the family take place in Jesus' life. Every year Jesus and His parents went to Jerusalem for the Feast of the Passover. When Jesus was twelve, however, He stayed in Jerusalem so that He could listen to the teachers in the temple courts. His parents assumed that Jesus was traveling with other family members and for a full day did not know that He was not with them. Once they knew He was missing, they went back to Jerusalem and searched the city for three days before they found Him in the temple. Notice His parents' response to the situation:

> When his parents saw him, they were astonished. His mother said to him, "Son, why have you treated us like this? Your father and I have been anxiously searching for you."
> "Why were you searching for me?" he asked. "Didn't you know I had to be in my Father's house?" But they did not understand what he was saying to them.
> Then he went down to Nazareth with them and was obedient to them. But his mother treasured all these things in her heart. And Jesus grew in wisdom and stature, and in favor with God and men.
>
> Luke 2:48–52

Jesus created some turmoil in His family when He went off and did what He had to do! He had reached a point in his life where He needed to be with the teachers of the Scriptures. He was no longer a boy. Led by God the Father, He was taking a step away from the world of his parents toward the world of men. This step did not please His parents. They did not understand it and were worried about Him. However, this step was necessary if Jesus was to continue to grow "in wisdom and stature, and in favor with God and men."

At some point, the normal spiritual and psychological development of a boy requires a movement beyond the world of his parents. In order to develop fully as a man, a young man needs to become more independent of his parents and step into his place in the world of men. The Christian community of men can play an important role in directing and nurturing this difficult stage of a young man's life.

Initiation Moves a Man From One Stage of Life Into Another

In order to develop their full potential, men need to be prepared for and led through the various stages of life. When a man marries, his life is different from what it was when he was single. When a man owns a large company, he faces different demands from those he faced as a teenager when he took his first job. When he becomes a father, a man relates to his children in a different way than he relates to the children who live in his neighborhood. A man who receives nurturing and encouragement as he develops through these stages of life is fortunate.

A series of events in David's life shows his progress in becoming a man. Like Samuel, he also had a clear initiation into manhood, a clear setting apart from his family. I find it interesting that Samuel was the man who initiated David into his adult role. This event occurred when Samuel anointed David to be the next king of Israel (see 1 Samuel 16:1–13).

God had directed Samuel to anoint one of the sons of Jesse, David's father, to take Saul's place as king of Israel, but did not tell him ahead of time which son to anoint. As the youngest son, David was his family's least likely choice—in fact, he was not even invited to participate in the selection process. One can imagine the pain he must have felt to not be remembered by his father. One by one, David's seven brothers stood before Samuel, but the Lord had not chosen any of them. Finally, Samuel had to ask if there were any more sons in the family. When David was brought to him, "the Lord said, 'Rise and anoint him; he is the one.' So Samuel took the horn of oil and anointed him in the presence of his brothers, and from that day on the Spirit of the Lord came upon David in power" (1 Samuel 16:12-13).

There was no denying the significance of what had happened in David's life when Samuel anointed him. But this was just the beginning. Samuel did not say to David, "You've been anointed, so let's tell Saul to take early retirement so you can take over." Instead, David continued his maturation process through a number of initiatory experiences and stages of life that eventually prepared him to become king.

One of the most famous of these experiences occurred some time later when David went to the battlefield to deliver food to his brothers. While there he encountered the giant, Goliath. Although David was experienced in fighting wild animals to protect his father's sheep, his battle with Goliath was his initiation as a warrior of Israel. When introduced to Saul's armor and weapons, David discovered they did not suit him. Instead he defeated Goliath with his sling and a stone. After his victory over Goliath, David spent many years fighting the enemies of Israel. This was an important stage of life that helped prepare him for his future role as king and protector of Israel.

David also spent time living in the king's household, serving Saul and being part of his daily life. During those years of close contact with the king, David learned much about what it meant to be a ruler. Early in his experience with Saul, David had a chance to watch a healthy, powerful king conduct the nation's affairs and protect the nation from oppressive enemies. Later, David also had the opportunity to see how not to be king. He saw a great king of Israel lose sight of God's calling and direction for his life, and David watched as Saul's character deteriorated before his eyes.

Other examples of initiation in Scripture demonstrate how a mentor can take an active role in guiding a younger man along into a new stage of development. On his second missionary journey, Paul took Timothy under his wing. For a time, Timothy helped Paul in his ministry. Then Paul left Timothy in

Ephesus with instructions to continue the work they had started. Timothy was quite young to take on the challenging responsibility of leading the church at Ephesus. Paul knew this and continued to mentor him from a distance. Paul wrote Timothy the two letters that go by his name in the Bible to help him know how to continue fulfilling the responsibilities of his new leadership role.

Eli also had direct responsibility for initiating younger men into God's service. Eli had failed to initiate his sons into their God-ordained role, which had dire consequences for the priesthood and Eli's family (1 Samuel 2:27-36). Eli, however, was faithful in initiating Samuel into his God-ordained role as a prophet of Israel.

Initiation Develops the Whole Man

One of the purposes of initiation is not only to prepare a man to assume his appropriate role through the different stages of his life, but also to nurture the growth of the whole man. When a man's masculine growth is nurtured, all dimensions of his being will develop more fully. For instance, we know that as a warrior David had great physical strength and endurance, but we also know that he had highly developed creative abilities. His skill at singing and playing the harp was remarkable and provided comfort for king Saul when he was troubled by evil spirits.

David's spiritual side is even more well known than his ability as a warrior and musician. His reputation as a "man after God's own heart" has stood throughout the ages. His psalms express an honest, vulnerable, deep, unfailing relationship with his heavenly Father. In his relationship with God, David holds nothing back. He expresses a full range of emotion and spiritual feeling— depression, praise, hate, sadness, shame, and joy. There is no doubt that David struggled with honesty and integrity, but even in his darkest times, he strives to maintain a direct and feeling relationship with his heavenly Father.

Older men play an important role in nurturing a man's professional and emotional development, and his spiritual growth as well. Part of this nurturing involves helping a man hear the voice of God. An event in the lives of Samuel and Eli illustrates this process well.

When Samuel was about twelve years old, he and Eli were going to sleep in their usual places in the temple. The spiritual condition of Israel at the time was weak, and visions and messages from the Lord were infrequent; but on this particular night, the Lord called to Samuel:

> Samuel answered, "Here I am." And he ran to Eli and said, "Here I am; you called me."
>
> But Eli said, "I did not call; go back and lie down." So he went and lay down.
>
> Again the Lord called, "Samuel!" And Samuel got up and went to Eli and said, "Here I am; you called me."
>
> "My son," Eli said, "I did not call; go back and lie down."
>
> Now Samuel did not yet know the Lord: The word of the Lord had not yet been revealed to him.
>
> The Lord called Samuel a third time, and Samuel got up and went to Eli and said, "Here I am; you called me."
>
> Then Eli realized that the Lord was calling the boy. So Eli told Samuel, "Go and lie down, and if he calls you, say, 'Speak, Lord, for your servant is listening.'" So Samuel went and lay down in his place.
>
> The Lord came and stood there, calling as at the other times, "Samuel! Samuel!"
>
> Then Samuel said, "Speak, for your servant is listening."
>
> 1 Samuel 3:4–10

On his own, Samuel could not discern the voice of God! He could not tell the difference between Eli's voice and God's voice. Only through the wisdom of Eli's experience did Samuel learn how to hear God's voice. I think this story has a powerful message for Christian men today. It shows the need for men who have experienced a lifetime of listening to God and drawing close to Him to help younger men discern God's voice.

Eli does not stop with helping Samuel hear God's voice. He then leads Samuel into another vital lesson that will help equip him to carry out his future role as God's prophet. Eli impresses upon Samuel the necessity of being honest and truthful, even when it is painful to do so. The message God gave to Samuel, however, is devastating to his beloved mentor and his family:

> "At that time I will carry out against Eli everything I spoke against his family—from beginning to end. For I told him that I would judge his family forever because of the sin he knew about; his sons made themselves contemptible, and he failed to restrain them. Therefore, I swore to the house of Eli, The guilt of Eli's house will never be atoned for by sacrifice or offering."
>
> 1 Samuel 3:12–14

Understandably, Samuel did not want to give Eli this unfortunate news. But he could never have carried out his future role as prophet if he had not learned to listen to the voice of God and to proclaim His word at all costs.

These are not the kinds of lessons a man learns on his own. None of these stages and aspects of masculine development occurred without the input of other men. Samuel had Eli who, over a period of years, helped usher him into his role as prophet. David had Samuel to whom he could run in his time of need. Timothy had Paul who ministered with him side by side and continued to instruct and guide him as he assumed tremendous new responsibilities. David had the opportunity to observe Saul when he was still a great king.

A man needs relationships with a variety of men throughout his life in order to continue his masculine growth. A man needs men who will initiate him through the stages of life, who will nurture the development of all aspects of his masculinity. This is no less true today than it was in biblical times.

CHAPTER 10

The Nurturing Role of Male Mentors

No father can possibly be everything to his son or fill every one of the needs a son has as he grows into the ever-changing roles required by his relationships to his family, church, profession and society. Since a maturing son has a real and legitimate need for guidance and support in all of these areas as he progresses through life, the son needs relationships with men other than his father who will help initiate him into adult life. A boy who is becoming a young man is fortunate indeed if he has relationships with older men who will help him in this way.

One of those vital relationships with older men is with a mentor. A mentor plays a critical developmental role in a young man's life. The right mentor can nurture every aspect of masculine growth, helping a young man develop his full potential spiritually, emotionally, and professionally. A mentor steps in to fill some of the needs a young man's father cannot fill and plays a key role in helping the son heal from the woundedness of his relationship with his father.

What Exactly Is a Mentor?

Samuel Osherson, a Harvard psychologist, has conducted

extensive research on male mentoring. Notice how he summarizes the mentor's role:

> A mentor is a more senior, usually older, person in the world of work who serves a transitional function for the young person, helping him to become established in the adult world of work yet also nurturing his own special values and beliefs. More people *think* they have mentors than actually do in the true sense of the term: a close *nurturing* relationship between old and young in the work world. Given the nature of the workplace, the mentor is usually a male, particularly for men.
>
> The mentor serves very important, healthy functions in helping the younger person mature into adulthood. Dr. George Vaillant has examined in detail the lives of successful men from college through later adulthood in what has come to be called the Grant Study. He found the presence of mentors central to men's career success and to their maturation as people. "The new role model of the late twenties and early thirties seemed associated with the acquisition of solid career identification." Men with relatively unsuccessful careers either had not discovered mentors until their early forties or had mentors only in adolescence.
>
> The mentee, too, serves an essential function for the mentor: By nurturing the younger person, the mentor keeps alive his own values and hopes, which helps him deal with his mortality and allows him to develop more "generative" parts of himself. Indeed, many men find that the mentoring relationship at work allows them to heal some of the wounds of parenting; feeling frustrated with their own children, some men turn to their younger colleagues as "surrogate sons."
>
> Daniel Levinson, one of the most careful students of the mentoring relationship, writes that "the mentor relationship is one of the most complex, and developmentally important, a man can have in early adulthood."[1]

I would add that the mentor relationship is important not

only during early adulthood, but throughout a man's life. No man ever outgrows the need for a mentor; in fact, men need many mentors during the course of life. A vocational mentor is essential for helping a young man find his way in the business world. Another mentor may be primarily spiritual. Another connects with a man and listens to his family concerns, helping him feel and respond to his wife's and children's emotional needs. Still another may step in as a middle-aged man contemplates a risky step, such as quitting his job in order to go back to school or planning a career change. A mentor who expresses confidence in a mentee may offer invaluable support as the mentor, in turn, reaches down to a younger man who needs his help. And so it goes, one man after another being initiated into different areas of life and then turning to mentor younger men.

What Does the Mentor Relationship Look Like?

One of my first encounters with a mentor was with my great-uncle, Bill Henslin, (the man I mentioned in chapter 8 who, late in life, was elected mayor of his Minnesota town). He was quite a man. Unafraid to make changes in his life, he was his own person but was also solidly rooted in his relationships with his family.

Bill gave me an incredible gift: the sense that he had as much time for me as I needed. In fact, he was that way with everyone. He never seemed rushed or hurried and always wanted to know how I was doing. As he asked questions about my activities and plans, his warm smile and lively, twinkling eyes clearly conveyed his sincere interest in me. When I finished high school and went on to college, when I married, when I pursued my first graduate degree, when I became a father, when I contemplated a move to the West Coast to earn my doctorate, Bill was always there. Without fail, he was willing to talk, tell a few jokes, and share a few struggles.

Each time I came to town, I would find Bill involved with people. He might be talking with a group of men at the grain elevator, in the tavern playing cards and drinking coffee, or at the service station. An old man with a deeply lined face, he had assumed the position in his community of chief encourager and listener. He had a way of connecting with just about every-one—a neighbor, the teenager in trouble, even the "very im-portant" people in town. A gentle, warm man who laughed deeply, Bill had an impact on everyone with whom he was involved. His kindness and warmth communicated to me much of what God must be like. When he placed that big hand of his on my shoulder and smiled, I knew he cared about me.

Bill showed me some of what it meant to be a successful old man. He had grown through the struggles, pain, and fears of life without destroying his relationship with God, his wife, or his children. He was faithful to the principles that governed his life. His rock-solid values never shifted, no matter what popular opinion might be. He was straightforward, and some-times blunt, in sharing his wisdom. At other times he would simply listen and stand by me, his quiet, mature strength being encouragement enough.

In college I met Dr. King, a solid Christian who became a mentor early in my professional life. He had an outstanding reputation among students. The word on campus was, if you had to take a psychology class, try to get it with Dr. King. My experiences with him taught me that it was possible to be a Christian and to be involved in the field of psychology.

Although he taught at a state university and could say little about his faith in class, Dr. King would often hum or quietly sing hymns as he walked about campus or waited for the classroom to fill with students. When classroom discussion centered on a topic that pointed to the need for spiritual insight, he would ask the students whom he knew were Christians to share their ideas. I deeply admired his ability to communicate the message of Christ within the limitations of his position. His boldness and genuine warmth touched everyone who had contact with him. I often met with him after class to talk about Christianity and how Christian beliefs fit in with psychology. He was a great help to me in the process of maturing as a man, as a Christian, and as a psychologist.

As I continued my schooling, my practicum supervisors also became mentors to me. Dr. Benedict Cooley expressed a warmth and deep caring that I had experienced only occasionally before in my relationships with men. The freedom and relaxed confidence he exhibited as he shared about his spiritual life with his clients also impressed me.

Dr. Klimek prodded me toward deeper masculine growth. He challenged me to look deeper, both into myself and my clients. He made it clear to me that my clients would be limited in their personal growth if I limited my own growth. He not only challenged me to grow, but through his own life modeled a deep commitment to ongoing personal growth. He also exhibited great confidence in his intuition and helped me become more confident in mine.

More than a professional mentor, Dr. Klimek was also a remarkable father. He was very much at ease with his children and had an unusual ability to accept their uniqueness while at the same time setting firm boundaries for their actions. The outer appearance of the family was less important to him than was his children's freedom to develop their individual personalities. When I spent time with Dr. Klimek and his wife, I noticed a deep warmth and caring between them; they seemed to genuinely enjoy being together. As I got to know him better, I deeply admired his actions as a man, as a husband, as a father, and as a therapist. He was a mentor to me in all of those areas.

When I moved to California to pursue my doctoral degree, Dr. Bill Hunter became another mentor in my life. He and his wife Florence worked at the school I attended and consistently offered emotional support. Their help at that time in my life was very important. My wife Karen and I had two small children, and I seriously wondered if I would be able to make it through the program and provide financially for my growing family. A man close to my father's age, Dr. Hunter deeply touched the little boy inside me. He listened to my worries and warmly expressed his confidence in me. His consistent encouragement helped me to hang in there and continue growing in my profession and in my faith in God.

During the past ten years, my most significant mentoring relationship has come through the experience of sharing an office with Willard Hawkins, M.D. Will has modeled excellence in his practice of medicine and has helped me learn what is involved in operating a financially successful practice. He has also modeled an unwavering commitment to tithing a portion of his earnings to God. Through Dr. Hawkins' support and guidance, I have grown in all of these areas. Yet he has provided much more than advice and a model of excellence. He has been able to listen to my deep feelings and respond to them in a way that encourages strength, boldness and confidence.

I feel privileged and grateful to have been mentored by all of these men. Each one offered his unique support, encouragement, accountability and wisdom that enabled me to continue growing in all aspects of my manhood. No earthly father could ever have given to me what these men together gave me. No man on earth can guide, direct and nurture another man in every area of life.

This was an important truth for me, and all sons, to learn. I have come to realize that I expected my father to be able to do everything—to not only love me but to teach me how to be a man, a husband, and a father and to nurture me spiritually, financially and professionally. Although the need for this kind of deep nurturing is real, it is not realistic or fair for a son to expect so much of his father. The nature of humanity is to be incomplete and needy, but only God can ultimately fill that deep neediness. To a certain extent, I expected my father to be to me what only God is capable of being. Only one Man, God's Son, has ever been capable of perfectly nurturing another man's development. Today, God's Holy Spirit ministers God the Father's healing and fulfillment through the support, encouragement and nurturing of His people.

So every man will benefit if he has close relationships with many "fathers" or mentors who will minister God's healing love to him throughout his life. In order to grow, every man needs to know that other men will be available to him during times of crisis. In order to step into new areas, every man needs to know that other men have gone before him and are available to guide him as he steps into the unknown.

A Mentor Ushers a Man Into a New Stage of Life

Mentors are crucial in helping men move into new stages of life. As a man moves from one stage of life to another, he needs an older man who will guide him toward his next steps of growth. He needs an older man who will teach him what he needs to know in order to be successful, who will confront him with the harsh realities he would rather ignore and say the hard things that challenge him to deeper personal growth. He needs an older man who will express confidence in the man he is and will become.

I'd like to share something with you that shows this type of mentoring in action, a section from Tom Clancy's novel, *Clear and Present Danger*. There is a particularly moving exchange between two characters, Jack Ryan, who is being groomed to head the CIA, and Admiral Greer, Ryan's long-time mentor who is dying of cancer. Their conversation takes place during one of Ryan's visits to Greer at Bethesda Naval Hospital.

He was barely a hundred pounds now, a scarecrow that had once been a man, a professional naval officer who'd commanded ships and led men in the service of their coun-

try. Fifty years of government service lay wasting away on
the hospital bed. It was more than the death of a man. It
was the death of an age, of a standard of behavior. Fifty
years of experience and wisdom and judgment were slip-
ping away. Jack took his seat next to the bed and waved
the security officer out of the room.

"Hey, boss."

His eyes opened.

*Now what do I say? How are you feeling? There's some-
thing to say to a dying man!*

"How was the trip, Jack?" the voice was weak.

"Belgium was okay. Everybody sends regards. Friday
I got to brief Fowler, like you did the last time."

"What do you think of him?"

"I think he needs some help on foreign policy."

A smile: "So do I. Gives a nice speech, though."

"I didn't exactly hit it off with one of his aides, Elliot,
the gal from Bennington. . . .

"Then you find her, and kiss and make up. . . . When
are you going to learn to bend that stiff Irish neck of yours?
Ask Basil sometime how much he likes the people he has
to work for. Your duty is to serve the *country,* Jack, not
just the people you happen to like." A blow from a professional boxer could not have stung worse.

"Yes, sir. You're right. I still have a lot to learn."

"Learn fast, boy. I haven't got many lessons left."

"Don't say that, Admiral." The line was delivered like
the plea of a child.

"It's my time, Jack. Some men I served with died off
Savo Island fifty years ago, or at Leyte, or lots of other
parts of the ocean. I've been a lot luckier than they were,
but it's my time. And it's your turn to take over for me. I
want you to take my place, Jack."

"I do need some advice, Admiral."

"Columbia?"

"I could ask how you know, but I won't."

"When a man like Arthur Moore won't look you in the
eye, you know that something is wrong. He was in here
Saturday and he wouldn't look me in the eye."

"He lied to me today." Ryan explained on for five minutes, outlining what he knew, what he suspected, and what he feared.

"And you want to know what to do?" Greer asked.

"I could sure use a little guidance, Admiral."

"You don't need guidance, Jack. You're smart enough. You have all the contacts you need. And you know what's right."

"But what about—"

"Politics? . . ." Greer almost laughed. "Jack, you know, when you lay here like this, you know what you think about? You think about all the things you'd like another chance at, all the mistakes, all the people you might have treated better, and you thank God that it wasn't worse. Jack, you will never regret honesty, even if it hurts people. When they made you a Marine lieutenant you swore an oath before God. I understand why we do that now. It's a help, not a threat. It's something to remind you how important words are. Ideas are important. Principles are important. Words are important. Your word is the most important of all. Your word is who you are. That's the last lesson, Jack. You have to carry on from here." He paused, and Jack could see the pain coming through the heavy medications. "You have a family, Jack. Go home to them. Give 'em my love and tell them that I think their daddy is a pretty good guy, and they ought to be proud of him. Good night, Jack."[2]

All men should be so fortunate as to have an older man who will share with them in such an honest and caring manner. One reason I enjoy reading all kinds of stories about men is because the interaction and nature of male relationships in the stories I read fascinates me. I think we can learn something about ourselves and our relationships by reading stories about other men, whether they be fiction or nonfiction. That is why I enjoy the stories of men and their relationships that are revealed through Scripture. These stories fascinate me and teach me so much.

To me, the story of David, the shepherd boy who loved God and became one of the greatest kings of Israel, is one of the most fascinating and revealing stories about male relationships. A number of events in David's life point toward a need for the kind of male friendships we have been examining in this book. In the previous chapter we looked at some of the initiatory events in David's life. Now let us look at the mentoring that took place in his life during a time of crisis.

Every Man Needs a Man to Run to in Crisis

For a time, things seemed to be going well in David's life. Samuel had anointed him king of Israel, the people honored him as their greatest war hero, he had married Saul's daughter who loved him, and he had found a loyal friend in Saul's son, Jonathan. The only problem was, Saul had gone off the deep end and wanted to kill him (1 Samuel 16:13–19:1). Saul's desire to kill David was so strong that even after he made a promise before God to let David live, he went back on his word. Notice how Scripture describes the situation:

> Saul listened to Jonathan and took this oath: "As surely as the Lord lives, David will not be put to death."
> So Jonathan called David and told him the whole conversation. He brought him to Saul, and David was with Saul as before.
>
> 1 Samuel 19:6–7

> But an evil spirit from the Lord came upon Saul as he was sitting in his house with his spear in his hand. While David was playing the harp, Saul tried to pin him to the wall with his spear, but David eluded him as Saul drove the spear into the wall. That night David made good his escape.
>
> 1 Samuel 19:9–10

Where did David go when he was forced to run for his life?

He went straight to the older man who first initiated him into the world of men and into the world of kings; he went to Samuel. First Samuel 19:18 says, "When David had fled and made his escape, he went to Samuel at Ramah and told him all that Saul had done to him. Then he and Samuel went to Naioth and stayed there."

This is a tremendously powerful passage of Scripture. David was a young man in desperate trouble. Samuel was a great prophet who was widely recognized as the man of God during this time in Israel's history. He commanded great respect and honor throughout the nation. No man would challenge Samuel because God was with him.

David instinctively knew he would find safety by running toward a man of God! When David ran to Samuel, he did not go with an agenda of what he wanted Samuel to do for him. David went to him for the safety, strength and connection with God that came from being with him. Can you imagine what it would have been like to have a holy man, a spiritual leader, like Samuel to go to when you faced frightening times during your early twenties?

When David and Samuel were together, David told him everything. He did not hold back. He related the entire story— everything that Saul had done. After David shared what was on his mind and heart, he and Samuel went to a different place and spent time together. I think their example reveals some important aspects of mentoring during a time of crisis.

Having support available during a time of crisis is vital to a man's continued growth. A man who does not have someone to run to operates out of fear and is unable to take positive steps of growth. When I began my practice, I needed a man like Dr. Hawkins to turn to. Beginning a practice is a scary and worrisome thing for anyone. You do not know where your clients will come from, how you will pay your office expenses, or if you'll have anything left to support your family. Even if you believe you are doing what God wants you to do, those fears and worries can overwhelm and paralyze you.

Just as David needed Samuel, every man today needs to talk to an older man who has made it through the struggles of life. Older men often have a deep sense of confidence and faith that God will indeed cause ". . . all things to work together for good to those who love God . . ." (Romans 8:28 NASB). During times of crisis, younger men need to be exposed to that strength of faith. They need to have an older man who can listen to their fears and respond—sometimes with a smile and gentle kidding, sometimes through a trusting prayer, sometimes with a confident challenge or encouraging advice. Sharing breaks the power of fear and enables a man to go on.

The extent and depth of support a man receives is directly related to the depth at which he shares what is on his heart. I think it is wise to remember that David told Samuel *everything*. It is hard to tell another man everything. Pride is such a big obstacle. Most men learn early in life that reaching out for help is a sign of weakness and masculine failure. More than anything else, men want to be viewed as real men, so it is easy for a man to feel embarrassed or shamed or to fear that his mentor will condemn him if he honestly tells the whole story, if he completely unveils his feelings. But if a man tells only part of the story, he will receive only part of the support his mentor can offer.

A young man will gain the most when he seeks out a spiritually alive mentor. One aspect of Dr. Hawkins' mentoring that has meant the most to me is his solid, consistent spirituality. I have been calmed and relieved by the many times he has prayed for me. I have been blessed as he has shared exciting things he has discovered in his devotional life. I have been greatly comforted in knowing not only that he would be there to support me in a time of crisis, but that he would also direct me toward a deeper relationship with God.

Samuel's spiritual benefit to David, and to the nation of Israel, becomes clear as their story continues. After baring his heart to Samuel, David stayed with him. When Saul found out where David was, he sent men to capture him (1 Samuel 19:19–20). Notice the impact of God's power that is conveyed through Samuel's spiritual leadership.

> But when they [Saul's men] saw a group of prophets prophesying, with Samuel standing there as their leader, the Spirit of God came upon Saul's men and they also prophesied. Saul was told about it, and he sent more men, and they prophesied too. Saul sent men a third time, and they also prophesied. . . .
> So Saul went to Naioth at Ramah. But the Spirit of God came even upon him, and he walked along prophesying.
>
> 1 Samuel 19:20–23

Can you imagine this scene? Saul sent men to kill David, but the power of the spiritual refuge David tapped into by being with Samuel overwhelmed those who came to destroy him! When faced with the decision to simply run away or to run to the wisdom, refuge and strength of Samuel, David chose to run to his mentor. Although David was a mighty warrior, he recognized his desperate need for support. I think David ran in exactly the right direction!

When facing a crisis, the support of a group of men is tremendous. Another message I see in this passage of Scripture is the great potential of men who are united in the power of the Lord. The spiritual power of Samuel, David and the men who were with them was so strong that it altered the course of Saul's messengers. Their mission was thwarted, and they, too, were impacted by God's power. I think this is the most powerful men's support group recorded in Scripture.

It is hard to imagine what it means to have the support of a group of men unless you have shared that experienced but this passage comes as close as any to describing it. A man who feels protected and supported by a group of men is changed.

The support of a group of men enables him to make right decisions and follow positive directions that he would otherwise be powerless to pursue. This is why the support concept in twelve-step groups such as Alcoholics Anonymous is so important. The ability to share with and receive support from a group of men enables a man to live one day at a time without succumbing to his addictions.

Even Saul, whose heart was hardened against David and against God, was touched by the scene at Naioth. What was happening there was so powerful that it stopped him in his tracks. God's Spirit broke through to his heart, and he connected with God in a way that he had not experienced for many years. I do not think it was an accident that Saul made that connection with God while in the company of other men rather than when he was alone. I think this further illustrates how God works in the hearts of men through their relationships with one another.

Mentors Struggle Too

Although mentor relationships are necessary in a man's life, they are not without problems. As Samuel Osherson points out, some of those problems stem from the father-son wound:

> The mentoring relationship suffers from the same deficiencies and stresses as other male relationships, particularly those of father and son. Notwithstanding its positive aspects, men often act out in the mentoring relationship unfinished conflicts with their own fathers and families. . . . Some mentors can be unconsciously destructive of their charges, and some mentees can demand an unattainable or inappropriate love from the mentor, which also interferes with their work.[3]

Rod, for example, worked in an insurance office. Soon after he began working there, Jim, the owner, took him under his wing. Rod was ecstatic. Jim was a Christian who appeared to be successful in his work, his faith and his relationship with his family. Rod soaked up all the encouragement Jim could give. He modeled Jim's sales techniques and learned to provide not just good service, but excellent service. His client list grew rapidly and soon the parent company recognized Rod's accomplishments. Immediately after Rod received that recognition, Jim withdrew his support from him.

Rod was crushed. The little boy within him had thrived on Jim's praise and encouragement—expressions of approval that Rod had not received from his father. Jim's own father-son wound had led him to become jealous of Rod's success and unable to recognize the valuable contribution Rod made to the company. Jim began to sabotage Rod's efforts by neglecting to give messages to Rod and by holding up vital information Rod needed to bring in new business. The deep needs of their respective father-son wounds led to an explosive termination of their relationship.

Things could have been different for Rod and Jim if they had been able to develop some awareness of their father-son wound and to deal with the deep feelings arising from it. Rod needed to recognize the source of his need for approval from Jim. Jim needed to become aware enough of his feelings that he could recognize his destructive response to Rod. But it isn't easy for a young man to find an older man who can mentor on a feeling level.

The feeling, nurturing potential of a mentor is often what draws the younger man to him; yet many men, because they have not dealt with their own father-son wound, are not equipped to fulfill the younger man's expectation of being a feeling mentor. Many mentors are far more comfortable if they pass on professional skills than if they try to nurture the development of a younger man's full masculine potential. As a result, much of the mentoring that takes place in our society focuses on a man's vocation, but ignores his heart. One young physician describes his frustration with this type of mentoring:

> "I feel like there are mentors to show me how to be a surgeon in the old mold—completely dedicated to my work to the exclusion of everything else, inattentive to other people's feelings and needs, and willing to ruthlessly climb the ladder of success." The young physician stopped and thought for a moment, then plunged on:
> "But there aren't mentors, or at least I haven't found them, who can help me become a feeling, powerful man, as well as a physician."[4]

This lack of nurturing of the whole person is tragic, but understandable when we realize that most men (and therefore most mentors) also suffer from their own father-son wound. When a man has not delved deeply into his own pain, he has no connection to his own feelings and certainly cannot connect with another man's feelings. It is only natural that a man who suffers a deficit of feelings within himself would only be able to mentor on a professional level.

It is a tremendously powerful thing to be mentored by a man who is connected to the deep feelings of his heart and can therefore touch the heart of a younger man. In my church there is such a man. Roger is an excellent businessman and a highly committed Christian. He has been in a serious recovery program for a number of years. He runs his own business in such a way that he can devote one day a week to the business concerns of the church. When I counsel young men who are struggling in business, I ask Roger to meet with them.

These young men always have the same reaction to him. They say they have never met a man who is as successful as he is yet listens to their concerns with such warmth and understanding. Roger is able to share with them about the facts of business life and discuss the hard choices and decisions they must make as business operators. He understands all aspects of their situation clearly and shares his options succinctly, yet conveys no blame or judgment that makes them feel naive or stupid. Roger has this tremendous gift because he has a good recovery going. He is a feeling man who is not afraid to express his love or commit himself to supporting and nurturing another man.

Dr. Hawkins is a similar mentor to physicians in training who do a rotation in family practice with him. (I expect the physician Osherson interviewed would love to have had such a doctor as a mentor.) The young physicians learn his skill because they watch him work. Many of them become enamored with his ability to get to the heart of a problem and quickly diagnose and treat it.

But Dr. Hawkins does more than teach how to treat illnesses. I've heard him share some of his fears and concerns as a physician. I've seen him educate his students about dysfunctional families and the relationship between those family issues and disease. As he teaches, he also helps them become aware of their own feelings and family issues. Consequently, a strong bond develops between him and his students. The physicians in training have not just completed a family practice rotation; they have experienced a significant relationship with an older man. Perhaps for the first time in their lives, the little boy (or girl) inside those physicians has felt cared for and nurtured.

There is no substitute for a mentor who nurtures the whole man. I wish it were easy to find such men. Unfortunately, it is not. It takes work to find and develop relationships with mentors. Some of these men can be found in your church, others may be found in your workplace, and still others can be found in recovery groups. Look for men you admire who have a healthy focus on their emotional and spiritual growth, who have a deep respect for other men, women, and children, and who are not afraid of their feelings. Look for a man who touches a deep part of you and instills within you a desire to do, with God's help, as well in life as he has done. No man will be a perfect mentor, but many men can play a mentoring role as a man progresses through life.

Becoming a Mentor

Since there are no perfect mentors, they come in all types and ages. A man does not need to be eighty-five before he can become a mentor. In some ways a man is a mentor at whatever age he is. It is not so much a man's chronological age as his masculine maturity that makes him a mentor. A man who is willing to dip deeply into his soul and face the pain of his father-son wound has something to offer. A man who seeks, with his whole heart and soul, continued growth in his relationship with his heavenly Father has something to offer as a mentor. So does a man who is living out a solid recovery program. A man who is emotionally connected with other men, who lives life with a depth of feeling and awareness of its meaning, has something to offer as a mentor.

Becoming a mentor is a process that begins early in life and deepens as a man matures. My son Ben, for instance, is a kind of mentor to the younger boys in the neighborhood. These boys simply like to hang around him. He's the big guy on the block and they look up to him. They cannot wait for a chance to play basketball with him.

Ben, in turn, looks up to some college guys in the neighborhood. They come from a Christian family and are solid, feeling young men. They, too, come over to the house to play basketball. As they play, they'll talk about sports and girlfriends. By spending time with Ben, they affirm him and fulfill a mentoring role in his life.

Ben's youth group leader also plays a mentoring role in Ben's life and the lives of a number of Ben's peers. Although he is only in his early twenties, this young man has much to pass on. He has a deep feeling for Christ and models to younger men how to have a good time without drugs, alcohol, or sex. He enjoys crazy things like riding an ice block down a hill or mildly disrupting the girls' youth group with water cannons; yet he is able to share about the importance of staying true to Christ's teachings, even when it is difficult.

As a man continues growing in his masculine strength, he has more and more to give to younger men. When he steps into a mentoring role, he realizes he has learned something during his journey through life that is worth passing on. In so-called primitive societies, the older men may devote 60 to 80 percent of their time to the work of initiating and mentoring the younger men. To be able to do so gives an older man a deep sense of purpose and meaning. He can take his last breath knowing that his life has counted for something. He can share his successes, his failures, his sources of pain, and his experiences of suffering so that perhaps a younger man does not have to go through what he has gone through. In a way, a mentor sifts through the ashes of his life to find the golden principles and lessons that remain in order to pass those treasures on to the generations that follow.

CHAPTER 11
▲▲▲▲▲▲▲▲▲▲▲▲▲▲

The Healing Power of Male Friendships

Most men are experts at maintaining superficial relationships. They may have social connections with other men at work. They may enjoy a great time with their buddies on softball, bowling or basketball teams. They may even spend an amazing amount of time talking with neighbors about lawn fertilizer. It is rare, however, for male relationships to offer any degree of emotional or spiritual support that will help a man heal from his deepest wounds and challenge him to keep growing and developing as a man.

Male conversations usually focus on talk about work, sports, interest rates and politics rather than on the deeper issues of life that truly trouble a man. I am amazed by a man's ability to talk pleasantly about something superficial like how the football team is doing while on the inside he is feeling turmoil and distress. He might be contemplating an affair, feeling afraid that he'll remember yet another long-forgotten memory of abuse he received as a child, worried that his drinking is out of control, struggling with an addiction to pornography or prostitutes, be so deeply depressed that he barely makes it out of bed in the morning, or feel angry and distant toward God. Most men would not dare share such deep feelings with another man. Most men have not even had a close friend since they were in high school, college or the service.

This is truly a tragedy. According to some researchers, the lack of intimate male friendships is a major social problem in our society that significantly affects a man's psychological and physical health.[1] Men need friends with whom they can share everything. They need friends who will stand by them, offering support and strength in times of trouble. Every man needs a trustworthy friend who knows everything there is to know about him. These intimate, honest and vulnerable masculine relationships are necessary if men are to heal from their father-son wound and grow into mature manhood.

Rabbi Baal Shem Tov is credited with a saying that describes the kind of caring, committed, strong friendships every man needs: "To pull a friend out of the mire, don't hesitate to get dirty."[2] A man who has a friend like this is fortunate indeed, but few men today are blessed with the treasure of a true friend. Let us take a close look at a deep male friendship that is recorded in Scripture—the friendship between Jonathan and David.

A Bond Between Warriors

At the time David and Jonathan met, they had already proven themselves to be great warriors. No soft, palace wimps, they were identified as the outstanding war heroes of Israel. By anyone's standards they had earned their status as *real* men.

Jonathan was the son of the king of Israel, a protector of the nation. At one time he commanded one-third of Israel's army (1 Samuel 13:2). His courage and strength in battle were well known, as was his ability to inspire courage and loyalty in others. While the army of Israel was in hiding, afraid to do battle against the Philistines, Jonathan and his armor-bearer launched an attack against a Philistine outpost—a feat not even Rambo could pull off! Notice the courage, confidence, and spiritual conviction of their adventure:

> On each side of the pass that Jonathan intended to cross to reach the Philistine outpost was a cliff; one was called Bozez, and the other Seneh. One cliff stood to the north toward Micmash, the other to the south toward Geba.
>
> Jonathan said to his young armor-bearer, "Come, let's go over to the outpost of those uncircumcised fellows. Perhaps the Lord will act in our behalf. Nothing can hinder the Lord from saving, whether by many or by few."
>
> "Do all that you have in mind," his armor-bearer said. "Go ahead; I am with you heart and soul."
>
> Jonathan said, "Come, then; we will cross over toward the men and let them see us. If they say to us, 'Wait there until we come to you,' we will stay where we are and not go up to them. But if they say, 'Come up to us,' we will climb up, because that will be our sign that the Lord has given them into our hands."
>
> So both of them showed themselves to the Philistine outpost. "Look!" said the Philistines. "The Hebrews are crawling out of the holes they were hiding in." The men of the outpost shouted to Jonathan and his armor-bearer, "Come up to us and we'll teach you a lesson."
>
> So Jonathan said to his armor-bearer, "Climb up after me; the Lord has given them into the hand of Israel."
>
> Jonathan climbed up, using his hands and feet, with his armor-bearer right behind him. The Philistines fell before Jonathan, and his armor-bearer followed and killed behind him.
>
> 1 Samuel 14:4–13

What a leader Jonathan is! Led by the conviction that God would direct their actions, Jonathan and his armor-bearer embarked on what appeared to be a suicide mission. Without a moment's hesitation, the two men took a step of incredible courage and killed more than twenty Philistines (1 Samuel

14:14). Then God sent a panic through the whole Philistine army, and Israel was delivered from their enemies that day (1 Samuel 14:15-23).

Afterward, when Saul was ready to put Jonathan to death for disobeying an order that Jonathan had never heard, the men of Israel said, "'Should Jonathan die—he who has brought about his great deliverance in Israel? Never! As surely as the Lord lives, not a hair of his head will fall to the ground, for he did this today with God's help.' So the men rescued Jonathan, and he was not put to death" (1 Samuel 14:45). Jonathan was so well respected that the army of Israel was willing to stand against their king in order to protect him!

David, although not from the royal family, had been chosen by God to be king of Israel after Saul. Beginning with his contest against the giant Goliath, David, too, had earned a reputation as one of Israel's greatest warriors.

David did not set out to be a great warrior. His first visit to a battlefield was in response to his father's instruction to deliver food to his older brothers and to find out how they were doing (1 Samuel 17:17–19). As soon as David arrived on the scene, he was caught up in the tension, challenge, fear and excitement of battle:

> He reached the camp as the army was going out to its battle positions, shouting the war cry. Israel and the Philistines were drawing up their lines facing each other. David left his things with the keeper of supplies, ran to the battle lines and greeted his brothers. As he was talking with them, Goliath, the Philistine champion from Gath, stepped out from his lines and shouted his usual defiance, and David heard it. When the Israelites saw the man, they all ran from him in great fear.
>
> 1 Samuel 17:20–24

Can you imagine what it was like for David, a seventeen- or eighteen-year-old shepherd, to come upon this scene?[3] The

Israelite army had lived with the tension of maintaining a state of battle readiness for quite some time. Goliath had been issuing his defiant challenge every day for forty days (1 Samuel 17:16). Daily his words chilled the hearts of the weary Israelites, and they ran from him in fear.

Their fear was understandable. Goliath was nine feet, nine inches tall—definitely qualifying for any NBA team. He was a strong warrior, feared even by the Philistines. He wore a bronze helmet and suit of armor that weighed 125 pounds. The tip of his spear weighed 15 pounds.[4] Not even Saul, the king of Israel, would stand against him in battle.

David was different. At that time in his life, he had a close relationship with God. He probably spent many otherwise lonely hours in communion with God, sharing everything in his heart with his Heavenly Father and connecting with His sure reply. He was appalled that any man, giant or not, would defy the "armies of the living God" (1 Samuel 17:36). On the basis of his spiritual conviction, David decided to fight Goliath.

David's decision to take on the giant's challenge showed great courage, but his decision to fight without armor, without the traditional protection and weapons of war, is astounding (1 Samuel 17:32–40)! With a deep spiritual conviction similar to the kind Jonathan had shown in attacking the Philistine outpost, David moved onto the battlefield against Goliath. Just as Jonathan did, he faced the taunts of his enemy and conquered:

> Then he took his staff in his hand, chose five smooth stones from the stream, put them in the pouch of his shepherd's bag and, with his sling in his hand, approached the Philistine.
>
> Meanwhile, the Philistine, with his shield-bearer in front of him, kept coming closer to David. He looked David over and saw that he was only a boy, ruddy and handsome, and he despised him. He said to David, "Am I a dog, that you come at me with sticks?" And the Philistine cursed

David by his gods. "Come here," he said, "and I'll give your flesh to the birds of the air and the beasts of the field!"

David said to the Philistine, "You come against me with sword and spear and javelin, but I come against you in the name of the Lord Almighty, the God of the armies of Israel, whom you have defied. This day the Lord will hand you over to me, and I'll strike you down and cut off your head. Today I will give the carcasses of the Philistine army to the birds of the air and the beasts of the earth, and the whole world will know that there is a God in Israel. . . ."

As the Philistine moved closer to attack him, David ran quickly toward the battle line to meet him. Reaching into his bag and taking out a stone, he slung it and struck the Philistine on the forehead. The stone sank into his forehead, and he fell facedown on the ground.

So David triumphed over the Philistine with a sling and a stone; without a sword in his hand he struck down the Philistine and killed him.

1 Samuel 17:40–50

What a warrior! David's action led to a great victory for Israel. The people were overjoyed at their delivery from the Philistines' oppression and credited David with the victory. The women danced in the streets, singing, "Saul has slain his thousands, and David his tens of thousands." (1 Samuel 18:7).

Immediately after David killed Goliath, Saul spoke with David. Jonathan apparently was nearby, listening, for Scripture says:

After David had finished talking with Saul, Jonathan became one in spirit with David. . . . And Jonathan made a covenant with David because he loved him as himself. Jonathan took off the robe he was wearing and gave it to David, along with his tunic, and even his sword, his bow and his belt.

1 Samuel 18:1–4

This marked the beginning of the covenant friendship between Jonathan and David.

The Gift of Covenant Friendship

The relationship between Jonathan and David was no casual acquaintance. It was a deep, committed love relationship between powerful men. In fact Scripture says more than once that Jonathan loved David as he loved himself (see 1 Samuel 18:1-3; 20:17).

The depth of their commitment to each other was dramatically illustrated by Jonathan's gifts to David, which symbolized the deep level of respect, humility, trust and loyalty inherent in their relationship. Jonathan took off the items of clothing that symbolized his royal status as son of the king of Israel and gave them to David. He literally handed over the outward evidence of his status in the world to his friend. This is not something a man does lightly. It is even more amazing that Jonathan also gave David his weapons, his means of defense.

Even today men have a strong attachment to their weapons. Men who own guns seem to have no shortage of stories and praises to relate about their favorite pistols, rifles or shotguns. Boys rarely forget the first knife or .22 rifle they receive. When a boy receives such a gift, he feels as if he has gained recognition that he is more than just a boy. When he carries a knife around in his pocket or walks through the woods or fields with his rifle, he feels as if he belongs in the world of men. He imagines himself as a man, fighting off bears, mountain lions, and bad guys with the weapons in his hands. Can you imagine how much stronger a great warrior's attachment to his weapons would be?

This interaction between Jonathan and David is beautiful. Jonathan's gifts not only communicate his deep commitment to David, but David accepts these symbols of commitment without protest. He does not say, "Oh, Jonathan, you shouldn't do this. This sword is too valuable to give to me." It is not easy for a man to accept a gift of such depth from another man; yet the gift of covenant friendship is a gift all men need in their lives.

I experienced such a friendship when I was in my late twenties. While I was working at a mental health center in conjunction with a community effort to develop a group home for the developmentally disabled, I met Hal and Marion Lynch, whose youngest daughter had Down's Syndrome. Through our interaction at planning meetings, public hearings, and the like, we developed a friendship.

Hal, a successful banker, exemplified the values of hard work, honesty, and loyalty to God, his wife, his children and his community. I often met with Hal and Marion over lunch to discuss plans for the group home. I usually met them at the bank, then we would walk down the street to a small cafe. A curious thing happened to us almost every time we walked a few steps outside the bank. Marion would stop to say hello to someone she knew, and a few steps further on Hal would walk across the street to chat with someone he saw. Invariably we walked down the street in a crisscross fashion, eventually ending up at the cafe at about the same time! I will always remember how Hal and Marion warmly greeted each person they met and how they genuinely cared about what was happening in the lives of others. In Hal I saw a deeply caring and generous man who did much to support the people in his community in tangible ways, regardless of their status or depth of need. He was not afraid to commit himself and his resources to others.

It was not easy for me to tell Hal about my decision to move my family to California where I could go back to school to earn my doctorate. I was not afraid of his response, but it was hard to face the loss of moving away from such a good man and dear friend. When Hal learned that I was making the move without any assurance that I would have a job when I got there, he reached into his pocket and gave me five $100 bills. He then said, "Make sure, when you get to California and move into your house, that you and Karen use this money to buy something nice for yourselves." I took the money and immediately wanted to give it back because I did not feel worthy of such a gift. Hal continued, "And I want you to know that if you ever need money while you are in school, you just call us, and we'll send it to you."

When Hal said this to me, I began to cry. The little boy within me had never received a gift quite like this one—a generous gift with no strings attached plus a commitment to help me out whenever I needed it. I knew from experience that when Hal made a commitment, you could take it to the bank.

I needed money several times during graduate school and whenever I asked, Hal quickly sent it to me. When times were tough, it felt good to know that another man had such deep love and confidence in me that he was willing to verbally and materially support me whenever I needed it. When I got out of school, I paid Hal back first—not because he asked me to, but because I so appreciated his trust and commitment.

I have often wondered if what I felt in my relationship with Hal is similar to what David felt in his friendship with Jonathan. Jonathan was certainly a friend who was not afraid to commit himself wholeheartedly; he held nothing back. Their friendship was more than a happy camaraderie that overflowed in the ecstatic moments of victory. David knew that when Jonathan made a commitment to him, he would come through.

As their lives unfolded, David and Jonathan experienced situations that tested their commitment to one another and stretched the depths of their relationship. Their response to these difficult and painful circumstances shows how a covenant relationship with another man directs a man in his walk with God, enables him to share and resolve his deepest feelings and fears, supports him during his darkest hours, and develops his character. Let us consider the qualities of their friendship that promote healing for a man's soul and encourage his masculine growth.

Covenant Friends Are Loyal and Trustworthy

After their covenant of friendship was established, David and Jonathan continued to be warriors of Israel, fighting against the Philistines. David, particularly, met with great success. The people loved and praised him; but as David's popularity grew, King Saul became increasingly afraid of him. Saul did everything he could to thwart David's efforts and even tried to kill him (1 Samuel 18:8–30).

David was in a difficult position. He had done nothing but serve his king and country as best he could; yet he was both loved and hated. He was on an emotional roller coaster: first viewed as special by the king who later viewed him as an enemy, then being highly esteemed by the people while being pursued by a king who literally wanted to pin him to the wall. Perhaps David even wondered if his relationship with Jonathan, Saul's son, would survive this threat. If so he did not have to worry, for Jonathan was a man of deep integrity and unfailing loyalty. Notice how courageously he intervened on David's behalf:

> Saul told his son Jonathan and all the attendants to kill David. But Jonathan was very fond of David and warned him, "My father Saul is looking for a chance to kill you. Be on your guard tomorrow morning; go into hiding and stay there. I will go out and stand with my father in the field where you are. I'll speak to him about you and will tell you what I find out."
> Jonathan spoke well of David to Saul his father and said to him, "Let not the king do wrong to his servant David; he has not wronged you, and what he has done has benefited you greatly. He took his life in his hands when he killed the Philistine. The Lord won a great victory for all Israel, and you saw it and were glad. Why then would you do wrong to an innocent man like David by killing him for no reason?"

Saul listened to Jonathan and took this oath: "As surely as the Lord lives, David will not be put to death."

So Jonathan called David and told him the whole conversation. He brought him to Saul, and David was with Saul as before.

1 Samuel 19:1–7

Who could ask for a more courageous friend than Jonathan? There is no doubt about where his loyalty resides. He is willing to risk his own reputation and safety in order to protect his friend. Saul's hatred of David was growing, and his behavior was becoming increasingly manipulative, violent and unpredictable. There was no guarantee that Saul would respond positively when Jonathan spoke well of David. In fact, Jonathan's actions exposed him to real personal risk.

The character traits of loyalty and trustworthiness seem almost endangered among men today. As families continue to be destroyed by dysfunctional behavior and a culture that has lost its basic, biblical values, loyal and trustworthy men become harder and harder to find. The problems and addictions of each successive generation produce fewer men who model these important qualities of character for the younger men; yet men of all ages hunger for relationships with men who live by these values, no matter what the cost.

An incident in pastor Stuart Briscoe's life illustrates this well. After he got out of the service, Stuart took a job in a bank. He worked hard and took on additional responsibilities, and soon one of the bank executives noticed him. This particular executive had a reputation for periodic rages and unreasonable demands. Bank employees dreaded interaction with him and hoped they would never have to work for him. This executive became Stuart's new boss.

Stuart had not been on the job long when he received a call for his boss. When Stuart conveyed the message, his boss told him to tell the customer he was not in. Stuart realized he was being asked to lie. So he mustered his courage, fully realizing that he might be yelled at and fired, and confronted his boss. "If I agree to lie for you now," he said, "you will never know if you can really trust me. Wouldn't you like to have one employee who you know will not lie for you—and most likely will not lie to you?"

Stuart's response stopped his boss in his tracks. He looked at Stuart for a moment, then agreed to take the call. His boss realized that he was dealing with a man of integrity and principle—a man who was loyal and trustworthy.

We need many such men in our world today. Men who are loyal and trustworthy make good friends. True friendship cannot exist apart from these characteristics. A man who wants to grow deeply in the character traits of loyalty, integrity and trustworthiness needs to seek out relationships with such men. Covenant friendship builds on these character traits and enables men to continue maturing in these areas throughout their lives.

Covenant Friends Trust Enough to Be Vulnerable and Are Committed Enough to Work Through Their Conflicts

Loyalty and trust are fundamental parts of true friendship, but the trying circumstances of life may at times put them to the test. As friends face these circumstances together, the depth of their loyalty and trust is revealed. If the friendship is true, friends learn that they can safely share their deepest emotions, even their most intense frustrations and greatest fears, and work through whatever conflicts may arise. This happened to David and Jonathan not long after Jonathan intervened to save David from Saul.

For a time life seemed to return to normal and go well for David. He continued to battle the Philistines when necessary and spent time at home, playing the harp for Saul. But life did not give David much breathing room. Suddenly his life turned upside down again:

> But an evil spirit from the Lord came upon Saul as he was sitting in his house with his spear in his hand. While David was playing the harp, Saul tried to pin him to the wall with his spear, but David eluded him as Saul drove the spear into the wall. That night David made good his escape.
>
> 1 Samuel 19:8–10

Picture David calmly playing after-dinner music for the king when suddenly Saul tries to skewer him! From this point on, David does not take any chances. His wife, Michal (Saul's daughter), helps him escape. After spending time with Samuel, his spiritual mentor, David goes straight to Jonathan, his friend.

This is no casual, let's-talk-about-the-good-old-days social visit. David is frustrated, angry, and frightened. He meets Jonathan and says, "What have I done? What is my crime? How have I wronged your father, that he is trying to take my life?" (1 Samuel 20:1).

Apparently Saul's recent attempt on David's life is news to Jonathan. "'Never!' Jonathan replied. 'You are not going to die! Look, my father doesn't do anything, great or small, without confiding in me. Why would he hide this from me? It's not so!'" (1 Samuel 20:2).

It is risky to share such deep and painful feelings. When men share what is truly in their hearts, they may be misunderstood and conflict may arise in their relationship. That is what happened during this interaction between David and Jonathan. David tells Jonathan that Saul tried to kill him, and Jonathan essentially tells David that it is not true. Conflict like this tests a friendship. No one quite knows how the conflict will be resolved.

But we must remember that David and Jonathan shared a sacred covenant. Their friendship was built on more than their feelings toward one another; it was built on a deep commitment that was made before God and sealed by Jonathan's symbolic gifts to David. Instead of brushing off the problem and distancing themselves from one another, David and Jonathan go deeper and deal with the tough reality of life. Notice how David responds to Jonathan's denial:

> But David took an oath and said, "Your father knows very well that I have found favor in your eyes, and he has said to himself, 'Jonathan must not know this or he will be grieved.' Yet as surely as the Lord lives and as you live, there is only a step between me and death."
>
> 1 Samuel 20:3

David does not mince any words here. He reveals the hard truth in a way that Jonathan cannot deny. David makes his statement under oath, and Jonathan knows that David would never lie under these circumstances. David affirms Jonathan's loyalty by telling him that the truth has been kept from him because of his unfailing friendship with David. David is not afraid to tell Jonathan the truth about Saul, even though his words must have been a painful reminder to Jonathan of the depth of his wound with his father Saul. David also is not afraid to admit to his friend that he is as good as dead.

David's words must have touched Jonathan deeply, for his reply was simple: "Jonathan said to David, 'Whatever you want me to do, I'll do for you'" (1 Samuel 20:4).

Vulnerability had been a characteristic of this relationship from the beginning. At the outset, when Jonathan gave his weapons to David, he was completely defenseless and vulnerable. David possessed the means of Jonathan's protection and could have killed him with his own sword. When his life was threatened by his friend's father, David came to Jonathan and, by honestly exposing everything in his heart, became vulnerable to Jonathan. David's fate was now in Jonathan's hands, and his friend responded by honoring that trust. He committed himself to do whatever was necessary to protect David.

This type of complete vulnerability is essential in a covenant friendship between men. Vulnerability includes a willingness to talk about and deal with dark aspects of life. It also means being honest enough to share and accept one another's deepest fears. Vulnerability and trust are necessary if men are to work through conflicts in their relationships. If one man holds back or is not trustworthy, the relationship is not safe. When men have a deep commitment to one another and are vulnerable enough to be truly honest with one another, healing can take place in their lives.

Covenant Friends Share and Work Through Their Deepest Feelings

After his time with Samuel, David went to Jonathan to share what was happening and to let off some steam. He needed Jonathan to hear him out, to give him some perspective on what was happening in his life. David knew he had done nothing but good in all of his dealings with Saul. He had put his life on the line numerous times as he served his king, God and country. Yet when David least expected it, Saul had attacked him.

In one way or another, these kinds of things happen in the lives of many men. It is not unusual for a man to be a victim of unjust anger from his boss, wife, parents or others. It is not unusual for unpredictable situations to generate fear or worry deep in a man's heart. When feelings of anger, fear, frustration, worry, resentment, sadness and hurt well up in a man, he needs a friend (or group of friends) with whom he can share those feelings. It is not good for a man to be alone with those feelings. Just as David needed to share his feelings with Jonathan, men today need to share their feelings with one another.

Consider the situation Andy faced because he worked for a man who was an alcoholic. Whenever this man drank too much, everyone in the office was on pins and needles. The boss's expectations were unreasonable. His constant demands created an atmosphere of chronic tension. Minor mistakes resulted in major blowups. Andy lived with nearly constant stomach pain and tension headaches, so by the time he arrived home at night, after nearly ten hours of tension and anxiety, his wife and family faced a six-foot bundle of raw nerves. He was like a coiled spring, ready to explode if he had to deal with any more tension.

One night, as he walked into the house, his eight-year-old son greeted him with the words, "Daddy, can you fix my bike? The chain fell off."

Andy turned toward him and yelled, "Do you expect me to fix everything around here?"

No sooner were the words out of his mouth than Andy realized he had brought the monster from work home with him. With horror he saw tears well up in his son's eyes. Since Andy had begun to realize how the little boy within him was being wounded at work, he could see how he had wounded his son. As tears filled his own eyes, he knelt down, held his son close, and told him he was sorry. Then he took his son's hand and together they walked into the garage to fix the bike.

When a man locks up his deep feelings of hurt, the people closest to him, usually his wife and children, become the unfortunate victims of the pain he carries inside. If a man truly desires to be a real man—the kind of husband and father his family needs—he has to be able to share with another man the deep, hurtful feelings he carries inside. Like David, men today need a safe place where they can share their feelings of woundedness and know that they are heard. Like David and Jonathan, men today need to wrestle through their feelings with another man.

David openly and directly expressed his raw emotions of frustration, fear, anger and injustice. Jonathan listened to him and offered a comforting perspective. Unfortunately, Jonathan's perspective was flawed, so David came back at him with a jarring dose of reality. David's words brought his friend back on track, forcing him to realize that assurances could do nothing to lessen the threat against David's life. Only then were Jonathan and David ready to deal with the situation at hand. Together they planned a solution that they could not have accomplished on their own.

This is a wonderful example of the deep healing of the masculine soul that can take place through covenant friendship. There is no doubt in my mind that men today need these kinds of relationships. These relationships can develop between friends or between men in a twelve-step support group. The important thing is, covenant relationships enable men to share their deep feelings, challenge men to stay focused on reality rather than drifting off into their fantasies, and help men deal in positive ways with whatever crises they may face. Let us see where the vulnerability and commitment between Jonathan and David takes them.

Covenant Friends Offer Unwavering Support

When Jonathan told David that he would do whatever David wanted him to do, he meant *anything*. His commitment came from the depths of his soul. They both knew his commitment could be costly. (After all, Jonathan's father had tried to kill David.) Once Jonathan reaffirmed their commitment, David presented his immediate problem and plan to him:

> So David said, "Look, tomorrow is the New Moon festival, and I am supposed to dine with the king; but let me go and hide in the field until the evening of the day after tomorrow. If your father misses me at all, tell him, 'David earnestly asked my permission to hurry to Bethlehem, his

hometown, because an annual sacrifice is being made there
for his whole clan.' If he says, 'Very well,' then your servant is safe. But if he loses his temper, you can be sure
that he is determined to harm me.

1 Samuel 20:5–7

David was in a precarious position. Even with their commitment to one another, it was not easy for these friends to deal
with the strong feelings that arose between them. They had to
continue to probe one another, expressing their feelings to see
how they were being received. After presenting his plan, David
said:

"As for you show kindness to your servant, for you have
brought him into a covenant with you before the Lord. If I
am guilty, then kill me yourself! Why hand me over to
your father?"
"Never!" Jonathan said. "If I had the least inkling that
my father was determined to harm you, wouldn't I tell you?"
David asked, "Who will tell me if your father answers
you harshly?"

1 Samuel 20:8–10

David knows the pressure Jonathan will be under to carry
out this plan. He knows the risk of being betrayed by his friend
and the risk Jonathan faces in his relationship with Saul. This
is not an easy friendship for them to continue, for it could lead
to death for one or both of them. In the face of imminent
danger, they reach down deep into the core of their emotions
and spiritual commitment and reaffirm their relationship before God:

Then Jonathan said to David: "By the Lord, the God of
Israel, I will surely sound out my father by this time the
day after tomorrow! If he is favorably disposed toward
you, will I not send you word and let you know? But if my
father is inclined to harm you, may the Lord deal with me,

be it ever so severely, if I do not let you know and send you
away safely. May the Lord be with you as he has been
with my father. But show me unfailing kindness like that
of the Lord as long as I live, so that I may not be killed,
and do not ever cut off your kindness from my family—not
even when the Lord has cut off every one of David's enemies from the face of the earth."

So Jonathan made a covenant with the house of David,
saying, "May the Lord call David's enemies to account."
And Jonathan had David reaffirm his oath out of love for
him, because he loved him as he loved himself.

1 Samuel 20:12–17

Can you imagine what it would mean to have a relationship
like this? Saul is the most powerful man in Israel. Men go into
action at his command, whether it be to play music, go to war,
eat dinner or kill someone. As Saul becomes more intent on
killing David, Jonathan's position becomes increasingly risky;
yet Jonathan does not withdraw from David for his own safety.
He sticks right in there with him, no matter how tough it gets.

In keeping with the precarious situation they face, both
men reaffirm their commitment to one another. This is an
important thing for men to do during trying times. When a
man deals with great pain, shameful feelings, or great risk, he
needs to know if his friend is still with him. If a man senses
that his friend's commitment is wavering, the issue needs to be
addressed directly and honestly. There is no room for guess-
work in a crisis. A man needs to know if his friend will hang
in with him or bail out.

This need to reaffirm one's commitment is not a question of a
man's integrity or honor. There was no doubt about the integrity
or honesty of Jonathan or David, but they still needed to verify
the depth of their commitment as the situation became more
serious. When men deal with serious situations, one of them may
reach a point where he can risk no more. The fear of abandonment or rejection is something that all men fear. Covenant

friends need to ask where they stand and continue deepening their commitment as their relationship grows. That is what Jonathan and David did as they faced the crisis before them.

Covenant Friends Watch Out for One Another, Even When the Risk Is Great

The first night of the New Moon festival passed without incident. Saul noticed that David was absent, but said nothing (1 Samuel 20:24–26). But when David was absent the second night, the crisis blew wide open. Saul asked Jonathan why David was not there, and Jonathan replied exactly as David had asked him to (1 Samuel 20:27–29). The worst scenario that David and Jonathan had imagined followed:

> Saul's anger flared up at Jonathan and he said to him, "You son of a perverse and rebellious woman! Don't I know that you have sided with the son of Jesse to your own shame and to the shame of the mother who bore you? As long as the son of Jesse lives on this earth, neither you nor your kingdom will be established. Now send and bring him to me, for he must die!"
> "Why should he be put to death? What has he done?" Jonathan asked his father. But Saul hurled his spear at him to kill him. Then Jonathan knew that his father intended to kill David.
>
> 1 Samuel 20:30–32

Every man needs a friend like Jonathan who is willing to go to the wall for him. Once again, Jonathan tried to bring Saul back to reality with the truth about David's goodness. He boldly stood up against his father's unrighteous hatred, in firm opposition to what was wrong, no matter what the price. He nearly paid for this loyalty with his life.

Every man needs other men in his life who will stand by him and watch his back. Men who are in combat together work as a unit, each watching out for the other. When a man goes into battle, it means a lot to know that he can count on his buddies when the going gets tough. Men need this kind of support, not only in battle but in everyday life.

Al, for example, experienced several years of incredible success in his job. His work greatly benefited the corporation he worked for, but he did not know that his division manager felt threatened by his success. Al's close friend, Ted, however, had heard Al's division manager make derogatory comments about Al's work to the company president. It was apparent to Ted that the division manager was setting Al up to be fired, so Ted told Al all that he had heard and suspected.

Al understood what was at stake and began sending the company president duplicate copies of the reports he was sending to his division manager. Before long, the company president recognized the division manager's game and fired him. The president then promoted Al to division manager. Al was fortunate to have a friend who let him know he was about to be attacked.

A man's enemies are not always external, however, and another type of watching out for one's back takes place in covenant friendships. It too carries significant risk—the risk of losing the friendship. The story of Ray and Jim shows what it means to go to the wall for a friend in a different way.

Jim cared deeply for Ray. They had known each other for years and had shared about the ups and downs of business and family life with each other many times. One thing about Ray bothered Jim, however. He had observed that Ray's social use of alcohol had become a regular part of his daily life, and Jim thought he recognized several symptoms of alcoholism in Ray's behavior. Still, Jim did not know what, if anything, he should say to his friend.

Jim's course of action became clear to him at a party in his home. Jim noticed a strong smell of alcohol on Ray's breath when he first arrived. As the evening progressed, Ray was a little louder than usual and a couple of times his behavior was out of control, causing others at the party to feel uncomfortable. As Jim thought about what he had seen in Ray's behavior that evening and over the past few years, he became certain that Ray was an alcoholic. Jim also connected this alcoholism to what had been happening in Ray's business. Although generally a solid businessman, Ray had made a series of bad decisions during the past year—decisions that seemed out of character and that were directing his business toward financial trouble. In light of this evidence, Jim decided he had to confront his friend.

It was not easy for Jim to talk to his friend about his concerns. To do so would mean risking many years of friendship. But as Ray's friend, he knew he could not sit back and watch Ray's health decline, his marriage deteriorate, and his business fail. Ray listened quietly as Jim explained what he had observed. When Jim was finished, Ray tearfully acknowledged that he could not control his drinking and did not know what to do. With Jim's support, Ray took positive steps to get help for his problem. By bringing this difficult issue out in the open, Jim went to the wall for his friend.

Jim was fortunate that his efforts to be a friend no matter what were as painless as they turned out to be. Jonathan was not as fortunate. The incident with Saul at the New Moon festival deeply wounded Jonathan. His worst nightmare had come true: his own father had shamed him in public and then tried to kill him. Jonathan did not eat for the remainder of the day. Despite his personal pain, Scripture says that Jonathan's reason for fasting was "because he was grieved at his father's shameful treatment of David" (1 Samuel 20:34).

Covenant Friends Keep Confidences

What an incredible friend Jonathan had proven himself to be. He was willing to risk even his life for his friend. Early the next morning, he set out to keep his commitment to reveal the bad news to David. This part of the story reveals yet another quality that is essential in a covenant relationship—absolute confidentiality:

> In the morning Jonathan went out to the field for his meeting with David. He had a small boy with him, and he said to the boy, "Run and find the arrows I shoot." As the boy ran, he shot an arrow beyond him. When the boy came to the place where Jonathan's arrow had fallen, Jonathan called out after him, "Isn't the arrow beyond you?" Then he shouted, "Hurry! Go quickly! Don't stop!" The boy picked up the arrow and returned to his master (The boy knew nothing of all this; only Jonathan and David knew.) Then Jonathan gave his weapons to the boy and said, "Go, carry them back to town."
>
> 1 Samuel 20:35–40

It would have been easy for Jonathan to tell Saul everything he knew in order to save his own neck. The situation was tense enough that Jonathan would have felt relieved if he had shared some of the emotional burden he carried with another man, but he did not. Certainly the boy who chased arrows for Jonathan would have been intrigued if Jonathan had revealed the true intent of their excursion, but Jonathan told him nothing.

Scripture clearly states that only Jonathan and David knew of their pact to verify Saul's intentions and protect David's life. Their words were simple, but they say much about the depth of trust and strength between these two great men. It was absolutely essential that what David and Jonathan shared between them stayed between them.

Keeping another man's confidence is a sacred part of masculine friendship. The ability to keep a confidence inspires trust, and trust enables a man to share whatever it is that keeps him in bondage so that he may heal. A man cannot risk sharing what is in his heart unless he has the assurance that what he says will be kept in confidence. It is no small matter for a man to share deep feelings, dark secrets and hidden failures. When a man takes the risk to do so, he should not have to worry whether what he says will become common knowledge in his church, workplace or community.

Sadly, most men today have never experienced this level of trust in their relationships with other men. This is one reason I recommend that men who are in recovery become involved in a twelve-step support group. Confidentiality is an essential element in twelve-step meetings such as Alcoholics Anonymous and Overcomers Outreach. At the beginning of every meeting, those who attend affirm that what is said in the meeting stays in the meeting. Within the safety of a commitment to confidentiality, whether within a twelve-step group or within a covenant friendship, a man can safely share what is on his heart.

Jonathan and David shared a commitment to confidentiality, so they felt completely safe with one another. They could tell each other anything. Within the safety of their relationship, they were free to expose the deepest feelings of their hearts.

Covenant Friends Touch One Another on a Deep Level

After Jonathan gave David the promised signal, he sent the boy who was with him back to town. David had been watching them all along and when Jonathan was alone, David came out to meet him. Notice what Scripture reveals about their friendship in their last meeting:

> After the boy had gone, David got up from the south side of the stone and bowed down before Jonathan three times, with his face to the ground. Then they kissed each other and wept together—but David wept the most.
> Jonathan said to David, "Go in peace, for we have sworn friendship with each other in the name of the Lord, saying, 'The Lord is witness between you and me, and be-

tween your descendants and my descendants forever.'"
Then David left, and Jonathan went back to the town.
1 Samuel 20:41–42

Realizing that they might never see one another again, David and Jonathan make no attempt to hide their feelings. Their loss is almost beyond words, so they hold each other and cry. It is no secret that these two great warriors meant much to each other.

It is very healing to let these feelings out and to share them with another man. One of the moments in my life that I prize the most is a time when my father opened up and shared his deep feelings with me. I was a teenager at the time and had awakened earlier than usual. As I walked from the house to the barn to do the milking, it seemed important that I get to the barn as quickly as I could. This was an unusual feeling for me because, as a teenager, I was often less than enthusiastic about morning milking. As I walked through the barn door, I saw Dad leaning against a post, crying. When he saw me, he stopped and tried to hide what he had been doing, but I already knew something was wrong and asked him what it was.

"I almost lost your Mom last night," he said. He explained that she had experienced a severe allergic reaction in the middle of the night and could barely breathe. Dad had rushed her into town, awakened the family doctor, and driven as quickly as he could to the hospital emergency room. The doctor rode in the back seat with my Mom—scalpel in hand, ready to do a tracheotomy if my mother's throat tightened any more.

My Dad's tears, shameful as they were to him, gave me a warm feeling toward him. They showed me his deep feelings for my mother and the depth of the trauma he had just been through. His tears showed me that deep feelings were a part of life.

The sad side of my father's story is that he probably never shared those feelings with another man. The strong men of our farming community stored their feelings deep inside, rarely willing to acknowledge or share them. Deep feelings were expressed only during moments of extreme crisis, when sufficient stress defeated the usual coping mechanisms.

When men have the opportunity to develop deep covenant relationships, they no longer have to hide their feelings. The ability to share their deep, heart-rending emotions does much to help men heal from the woundedness within. As painful as their parting was, Jonathan and David were free to share the depth of their feeling for one another, which I am sure comforted that them in the days ahead.

Covenant Friends Share a Lifelong Commitment to One Another

The days ahead were not easy for Jonathan and David. David continued to hide from Saul, and Jonathan continued to fight the Philistines. Eventually Jonathan and Saul were killed in battle on the same day (1 Samuel 31:2–6), and David mourned their deaths. A number of years later, David became king of Israel and Judah. Despite all that had happened during those years, David never forgot his commitment to Jonathan: ". . . we have sworn friendship with each other in the name of the Lord, saying, 'The Lord is witness between you and me, and between your descendants and my descendants forever'" (1 Samuel 20:42).

This was a powerful commitment for Jonathan and David to make. What man does not worry about his family's future? A man cannot simply assume that his friends will take care of his family, especially when one man has been anointed to be the next king of Israel and the other man is the son of the present king. If a man's friends intend to care for his family in the future, this promise must be directly and clearly communicated. David and Jonathan made an absolute commitment to each other for as long as they would live.

After he became king, David kept his promise. His actions were contrary to what one would have expected, because it was not unusual at that time for a king to kill remaining members of an opposing royal family. However, David located Mephibosheth, a crippled man and the only living son of Jonathan, and brought him into his household. "'Don't be afraid,' David said to him, 'for I will surely show you kindness for the sake of your father Jonathan. I will restore to you all the land that belonged to your grandfather Saul, and you will always eat at my table'" (2 Samuel 9:7). For the rest of his life, "Mephibosheth ate at David's table like one of the king's sons" (2 Samuel 9:11).

Today there is a crisis of masculine commitment. Will a man stay committed to his friends? Will he stay committed to his relationship with God? Will he stay committed to his wife? David and Jonathan exhibit what deep commitment really means—commitment not just during the good times, not just while they are together, but faithfulness that lasts as long as the man lives. We men today can learn from their example.

Covenant Friendship Makes a Difference in a Man's Life

I wish the story of David and Jonathan had a happy ending, but it does not. Scripture does not reveal that David had a close friendship with anyone other than Jonathan. Although David ruled well, his personal life deteriorated after Jonathan's death. He had an affair that resulted in an unwanted pregnancy. To cover up his sin David arranged for the woman's husband to be killed, then married her. The child born to them died a short time after birth.

In addition David, who had once revealed to Jonathan his great frustration regarding Saul's injustice, seemed unable to deal with wrongdoing in his own family. One of his sons raped one of his daughters, and David did nothing. Later, David's son Absalom killed Amnon, the brother who had raped his sister, because he could not handle the unresolved situation. In shame and anger, David rejected Absalom. This led to an irreparable wound between them that led to rebellion and war within his kingdom.

I think David's later life would have been very different if he had found another close friend like Jonathan. In a sense, David lost his way when Jonathan died. He no longer had a deep friend to turn to when he felt afraid or uncertain. There was no longer a person in his life who would risk everything for him and for whom he would do the same. He no longer had anyone who loved him unconditionally yet would tell him the hard truth and hold him accountable to it when necessary. There was no man in his life whom he could share his grief and his tears. When Jonathan died, David had to carry the burdens of his life alone.

I do not believe that what we men carry in our hearts today is much different from what David carried. David's story shows the healing power of covenant friendships and the impact masculine support can have on a man's life. It also shows what happens when that support is gone.

I think we men today have to ask the questions: Who is my friend? Who in my life can I turn to when I am in trouble? Who can I trust enough to share the deepest secrets and most painful hurts of my heart? Who will stand beside me and say, "I'll do whatever you need me to do for you?" Who will help me become the man God intended me to be?

CHAPTER 12
▲▲▲▲▲▲▲▲▲▲▲▲▲▲

A Vision for the Church as a Healing Community

I believe that the spiritual, emotional, and relational strength of men is the most significant untapped resource in the Christian community today. Although men assume the majority of leadership roles, such as deacon, elder or board member, women carry on the bulk of relational church ministries. Women are generally more involved than men in Bible studies, prayer ministries, service ministries and teaching ministries. They also usually lead the way in spiritual teaching within the home and make more of an effort to deepen relationships and communication between family members. I do not make these observations in order to criticize, but because they indicate the crisis of male involvement in the church and home. Our society today has come face to face with the consequences of the father's weak or nonexistent spiritual and emotional presence in the family. The church also faces a crisis in that it generally lacks men who are able to minister from the heart, who can relate to others not only on an intellectual level but on spiritual and emotional levels as well.

Imagine, if you will, what the church would be like if it were filled with men who had the same kind of commitment to one another that Jonathan and David had. Imagine how the church would be able to care for its members and the downtrodden of society if its men were able to feel deeply, to share their feelings of pain, and to freely express their compassion. Imagine how committed young men would be to God, to their wives, to their children and to the church if they were guided into manhood under the wise counsel of committed older men—men like Eli and Samuel. If Christians today are to fulfill this vision, we must discover what it will take to unleash the power and strength of the masculine soul within the church.

Healing the Hearts of Men

I am convinced that the key to unleashing this great masculine power, strength and feeling lies in the healing of the father-son wound. This great wound in the hearts of men blocks out deep feelings, prevents spiritually empowered living, and limits masculine growth. Through the process of healing from this deep wound, men become energized and activated. They are set free from spiritual and emotional passivity and begin to live lives of meaning and action.

Healing that enables a man to be spiritually and emotionally empowered requires the active involvement of other men. A man needs a community of men around him who will support and encourage him in his masculine development from birth until death. I believe the community of Christian men today—the church—needs to be doing this.

For a number of years, I have been involved in my own recovery program. I attend twelve-step meetings and have sought out deep relationships with a number of men. Some of these men are mentors, some are close friends, and some look to me as a mentor. I have made progress in dealing with the father-son wound in my life, yet some of the deep spiritual healing that has needed to take place has come only through the Christian community. Let me share an example of what I mean.

One of the big issues I have had to deal with is shame. The lack of direct expressions of love and care from my father and most of the other men in my family left me with feelings that I was never quite good enough to receive the affirmation I hungered for. The church I grew up in focused on outward behavior as the standard for acceptance. Since I could not live within the confines of its prescribed behavior and be a "good boy," I felt shamed by the church too. I am not seeking to place blame by revealing these things. The truth is, the men in my life had not experienced anything different themselves, so they did not know how to pass on feelings of affirmation and support. However, these strong messages of shame convinced me that there was more bad in me than good. During these years I carried that load of shame alone, never imagining that I could share those feelings with anyone—especially God who seemed cold and distant to me.

When I began attending First Evangelical Free Church of Fullerton, some of those old messages of shame started to crumble, releasing deep feelings within me. Many times the words of my pastor, Chuck Swindoll, touched my heart and tears would well up. Sometimes, just by listening to the music during worship my tears began to flow. At times I shed tears of sorrow, at other times tears of happiness. At first these powerful feelings embarrassed me, and I tried to hold them back. I just could not imagine a six-foot-five-inch man crying in church.

Then it occurred to me that perhaps the Holy Spirit was awakening me to an area of my feeling life that needed healing. If that were the case, then I was hindering His work by staying in shame and hiding my tears. So I decided that if tears came while I was in church, then I needed to let them come.

After I made this decision it became easier for me to hear and feel what pastor Chuck was sharing. I became more in tune with the deep laughter that came from the depth of his being. I was able to clearly hear the pain or the strong anger in his voice when he spoke about the evils of sin and the destruction it brought into people's lives. As my heart became more open to his messages, my image of God began to change.

You see, my father-son wound and earlier experiences had so distorted my image of God that I could only imagine God the Father to be a God of judgment, a conveyor of shame. If I did not do just the right things to please Him, or dared to expose to Him what was really in my heart, I was sure God would not want me around. To me God was a judge, not a God who felt sadness, compassion, love or pain. When I saw the life and energy that flowed through pastor Chuck as he shared what Scripture revealed about the realities of life, my relationship with God the Father began to change. Looking back, I now realize that God used Chuck Swindoll to touch my heart.

This is just one example of how the Christian community can help bring healing to the hearts of men. Men today bear a countless variety of wounds in their hearts. It takes strong relationships with father figures of all types—the company of men within the Christian community, as well as God the Father, God the Son, and God the Holy Spirit—to enable men to heal from their wounds and develop their full potential as men of God. This, of course, cannot happen without the strength and power of God's saving grace; but men cannot heal from the deep wounds in their hearts and develop their full, God-given potential without actively facing these issues. Men cannot do this alone, nor can their parents help them do it without the help of others. Every man, from birth until death, needs the support of a community of men who will enable his healing and nurture his full development through the stages of life.

A New Model for Discipleship

If the church is to activate the spiritual strength of its men, we need to expand our concept of discipleship. Traditionally, discipleship has meant training in the disciplines of Bible study, Scripture memorization, prayer and meditation on God's Word and instruction in the basic doctrines of the faith. Today, discipleship needs to be this and much more.

Discipleship must take place on a feeling level as well as on a thinking level. Some men cannot give in both these areas. A disciple who has not dealt with his own father-son wound, who is not connected with his feeling life, may be able to teach Bible study principles, but may not be fully equipped to help a man deal with his daily life and feelings in light of Scripture. Since there are no perfect "disciplers," every man needs several—each with his unique blend of strengths—to encourage him toward spiritual and emotional maturity.

We also need to change our idea of who can disciple. Even though we believe that everyone needs to be disciples, the expectations we have of those who disciple is shaming. Most of us are afraid to even attempt to disciple because we believe we almost have to be God in order to meet the expectations. We expect disciples to be able to open a Bible to the right verse instantly, to be able to explain all the cultural and linguistic nuances of every Hebrew or Greek word, to be able to recite the theological and doctrinal implications related to the verse, and to apply all of this perfectly in daily life.

We fail to realize that part of discipleship simply means one man asking another man how he is doing, receiving an honest response, and responding to that need from the depths of his heart and soul. It means that when a man's company is laying off people and he is scared he will lose his job, another man will sit with him and listen to his fears. Perhaps the man who listens will be able to share what God showed him during a similar crisis in his life, put his arm around him and ask what he can do to help or pray with him. When men have this kind of committed, supportive relationship with each other, spiritual growth naturally happens. This is discipleship in real life.

Real discipleship provides a path that moves a boy into deep, holy masculinity. In its most basic form, this kind of discipleship begins at birth. It means that older men, whatever their ages might be, care enough to invest themselves in the spiritual, emotional and physical lives of younger men. It means that older men will surround a boy as he becomes a man so that they can help guide and strengthen him through the stages of life and honor and celebrate his deepening status as a man of God.

A man needs to be a disciple spiritually and emotionally in order to discover his feeling life and to be healed from his father-son wound. This discovery usually does not happen on its own. Most men live without feeling much of anything until they reach midlife and cannot keep their emotions inside any longer. Left on their own, they will do almost anything to keep their feelings at bay—go out and get a new car, a new wife or a new job. They will try everything to avoid dealing with what is in their hearts.

Men need emotional as well as spiritual discipleship. If they lack this kind of nurturing, they will not be able to follow through in their lives and take action. This is why so many seminars and books on Christian marriage and parenting are wasted on men. Men absorb the information, but their hearts are not touched because they are so disconnected from their emotions. A man may read that he should spend more time with his kids, but unless he has felt the pain of his own father's absence, he does not really understand what his absence means to his children. A man may be told that he should do something special for his wife's birthday, so he may buy her candy and take her out to dinner. She may feel special for the moment, but she really wants her husband to respond to her inner feelings, to understand her world. When a husband begins to connect with his wife on a feeling level, he is able to give of himself in ways his wife really needs.

Spiritual and emotional discipleship touches the hearts of men. Until the hearts of men and women are touched, the ministry of the church is limited. When men connect with their feelings and begin to heal their father-son wound, they can have a powerful ministry. Let me tell you about Jim, a sixty-five-year-old man who got in touch with his feelings of woundedness and completely changed his life and ministry.

When Jim heard me speak about the father-son wound, he realized some important things about himself. Years ago he had gone to work in his dad's company in an effort to gain his approval. Long after his father had died, he had continued to keep the company going even though this was not what he really wanted to do with his life. When he discovered this inner motivation, he sold the company and retired. Then he began building bridges to his adult children, letting them know he was sorry that he had not been available to them when they were younger. Now he spends one day a week volunteering at the church and he teaches a Sunday school class for four-year-olds because he realizes that little children need older men to be active in their lives. He is always looking for opportunities to do things with his grandchildren. He also spends time each week distributing food to the poor.

This man has so much to give—and he is giving it! No one has to tell him he ought to be doing what he is doing; it just naturally flows from him. He was able to connect with his father-son wound, acknowledge his failures, and live a completely new, spiritually activated life. There is an awesome power at work when a man's heart is healed and he truly becomes spiritually alive.

Initiating a Man Through the Stages of Life

My hope for Christian men today is that they will become emotionally and spiritually activated so they can take steps toward nurturing and discipling one another in all aspects of masculine growth. I envision a whole community of men being available to initiate and support one another through all stages of life. I hope that a boy's life will be touched by men of all generations—older men, middle-aged men, and men in their early twenties—men who will show concern for him, talk with him, teach him and pray with him. Men of all ages need this kind of nurturing throughout life. I would like to share with you some examples of how this can be done.

When a young man graduates from high school, the men of the church could rally around him. They could acknowledge his entrance into a new stage of life and renew their commitment to be there for him as he gets older. Perhaps they could spend an evening with the young man and share some of the things they went through at that time of life—some of their fears, expectations and some of the ways they failed. By sharing their feelings and experiences, the older men could show the young man that it is not shameful to be afraid, that it is okay to fail, and that they are available to help him make it through the difficult times and to celebrate the good times.

Another opportunity to initiate a young man occurs when he gets a bit older and becomes serious about dating. During this crucial period the older men could take the young man away and talk with him about relationships with women and marriage. A young man needs the perspective of older men at this time in life. Most young men imagine a woman to be an all-loving, all-caring, all-sexual, all-nurturing, magical person. A young man needs to learn that no woman on earth will ever match up to what he thinks a woman is. He needs older men to bring some reality into his expectations.

Then, when a man is ready to get married, he needs the insight and wisdom older men can offer. A man needs, from the beginning, a long-term view of marriage. It is important for him to understand that marriage is different in your twenties, forties and sixties. He needs to know that a twenty-year-old's image of marriage will not last for a lifetime because each person has different issues to work through and each will change. He must realize that marriage is the foundation through which those issues are resolved and through which those changes occur. He needs to know that in marriage there are times of closeness and passion as well as times of coldness. He needs reassurance that when the passion dies down, it is no big deal; it just means that he and his wife have something to work on in the relationship. When passion runs low, it is not time to hire a divorce attorney, but is time to work on what is happening inside so that things will be okay again. Men who have been married for thirty or fifty years, as well as men who have been through a divorce, have something valuable to share with younger men.

When a man learns that he is to become a father, fathers of all generations need to gather around him, celebrate with him and disciple him in his new role. A man needs to adjust his expectations of his wife when children enter the family. He needs to understand that he will not always be first anymore. Men do not like that! Unless other men prepare him for these changes, a new father can become angry and jealous and behave like a little boy.

As a man's children grow up, he continues to require the guidance of other men. He needs to understand how his role in life will change as he matures. He will profit from the perspective of men who changed their attitudes toward work in order to have more time with their children, and he will learn from the hindsight of those who did not change. He needs to hear the pain in the heart of the father of a teenager who cannot talk to his son anymore because of the damage to their relationship. He will require an ongoing commitment of support and encouragement from other fathers.

When a man becomes a grandfather, he needs the guidance and support of other men as he assumes his new role. Other grandfathers can help him to learn how to be a grandfather, perhaps how to connect with grandchildren who live far away. Other grandfathers can help him understand what it means to be the husband of a grandmother. A new grandfather needs to hear the stories of younger men who had close relationships with their grandfathers—to hear them talk about the memorable times they spent with them.

Men need these kinds of initiatory experiences throughout life. These experiences should not be limited to the milestones of a man's family life; they need to include the turning points of his career and other interests as well. Prime times for initiatory experiences include a man's graduation from college, his completion of advanced degrees, his promotions in corporate or military service, changes in his career and his retirement. Initiation ceremonies can also recognize the milestones of a man's creative and personal development, such as the publication of his writings, his placement in an athletic contest, the acceptance of his work in an art exhibition or a host of other personal accomplishments.

A Lifetime of Support for Men in Need

Initiation provides the foundation through which a man receives ongoing support from the male Christian community. The initiation process awakens a man to the fact that other men can be a resource for him throughout life. It helps him realize that other men will be there for him as he works through his feelings, handles new situations and makes difficult decisions.

Men need this kind of support. Several years ago I was betrayed by a friend and business associate. This betrayal caused a great deal of pain and harm to me and others. My friend's actions produced one of the greatest wounds in my life and jeopardized a lifetime of work and diligence on my part. At the time I plunged into depression, fear, shame and worry. I doubted my ability to continue my work and seriously considered selling everything I owned, taking my wife and children to a remote part of the country, and finding some other way to support my family.

As you can imagine, I am not fun to be around when I am in that state of mind. I live on the verge of making bad decisions that could affect the rest of my life. I am tense and cannot sleep. Sadly, the people I love feel the impact of the turmoil within me. During times like these my only solution is to turn to God and to other men. Just as David needed Jonathan, I need men who are deeply committed to me and will stand by me—men who will help me work through my fear and worry and help me grow into a different spiritual, emotional and physical state.

I was fortunate to have had two friends who stayed close beside me throughout that horrible time. These men had every reason to abandon me, for my depression was deep and my feelings of shame were strong; but they stuck with me through the trouble, affirming me, encouraging me and strengthening me. They helped to set realistic boundaries with the friend who had betrayed me, identify the limits of my responsibility, and enabled me to see how I had overlooked my friend's dark side. As these two friends walked with me, the bond between us grew stronger, and God's ministry of grace became more real to me.

All men need relationships with other men who have what it takes to keep their commitments to each other during difficult times—men who are not afraid to be truthful and real. Many men carry deep, deep hurts that need to be healed. Sometimes a man begins to remember the sexual or emotional abuse he received as a young boy and feels as if he is losing control of his anger and fear. Sometimes a man loses his job and is so overwhelmed with shame from his past that he cannot bring himself to get out of bed in the morning and look for work. Sometimes a man reaches a crisis in midlife when he feels as if time is running short, so he plunges into a destructive whirlwind of adolescent-type activity.

In all of these situations and more, men need to be ministered to by other men. They need the support of men who will offer comfort in their pain and encouragement as they struggle toward healing. Ministering to another man may mean holding and comforting him when he has flashbacks of sexual abuse. It may mean gently listening to a man who for decades has never revealed the fearsome details of his darkest combat days in Vietnam. It may mean affirming a man who is apprehensive about making a career change. It may mean sharing tears with the man who helplessly watched his best buddy die following a mortar attack.

This is what I believe men's ministry is all about. Men are naturally afraid that other men will reject them if they share their deepest feelings and most intense struggles, so they keep their emotions to themselves for a long time. It takes a greatly hardened heart and/or tremendous amounts of alcohol, drugs, food, work or sex to keep these feelings locked inside. The ongoing ministry of a community of Christian men can do much to help men heal from the wounds in their hearts—old wounds as well as new. It can help them grow more fully into Christian manhood can help them put into action what Christ planted in their hearts when they became Christians.

My Hope for the Church

This is an exciting time to live within the Christian community. During the past five to ten years a movement has begun within the church. We have been changing how we view ourselves, how we relate to Scripture, and how we go about life and ministry. Our fundamental belief that Jesus Christ is the Son of God, our Lord and Savior, remains unshakable. It is a great comfort to have the sound principles of Scripture to guide us in an ever-changing and increasingly confusing world. It has also become apparent that God would have His people open their hearts to His loving touch and to one another.

The last words of the Old Testament speak of healed hearts:

> Behold, I am going to send you Elijah the Prophet before the coming of the great and terrible day of the Lord.
> And he will restore the hearts of the fathers to their children, and the hearts of the children to their fathers . . .
> Malachi 4: 5–6, (NASB)

The crises we face in the family, the church and society make it apparent that the hearts of fathers must be restored to their children and that the hearts of children must be restored to their fathers. For several reasons, I believe the Christian community is the place for this to happen.

First, the Christian community is one of the few communities left in our society. At one time people were born, lived and died in the same towns or neighborhoods. Today that rarely happens. Even today's families do not provide the sense of community they once did. Present divorce rates mean that many children grow up with several sets of grandparents, parents and siblings. The church is the one community that can provide people with an identity, and a place to learn and grow from birth until death.

Second, the church provides a common standard of values and beliefs that are based on the authority of Scripture. Although a common standard of values existed in our culture fifty years ago, there is no longer a culturally accepted moral authority. Fifty years ago most people—Christian or not—would agree that it was wrong to have an extramarital affair. Today many people do not even recognize the need for or legitimacy of moral authority. As society continues to disintegrate, the church is the only community of people who are willing to live life according to the unchanging principles of Scripture.

Third, God has always viewed His people as a community and as a family. The earthly father's role is important, but no father can be everything for his son. A son needs an incredible number of "fathers" in his life. This is where the men of the Christian community can step in and make a tremendous difference.

When men start allowing God to touch their hearts, and when they start reaching out to touch the hearts of other men, they will make a tremendous difference in the church and in the community as well. When men become actively involved in touching the hearts and lives of other men, they start helping one another, listening to one another and praying with one another. They begin to look forward to spending time together and start taking an active role in the church. Men who are spiritually activated take the living gospel into their communities. They reach out to the homeless and feed the hungry. They repair the widow's leaky roof. They become involved in the lives of boys who do not have a strong connection with their fathers. When men become spiritually activated, men's ministry means much more than golf tournaments and steak frys, because spiritually activated men are empowered to minister to others from the depths of their hearts.

I would like to leave you with a story about a spiritually empowered man.

A new pastor came to a church that had become close-minded and had lost its zeal for winning souls. He convinced them that God wanted them to begin an active outreach to the community around them, starting with the junior college across the street. Some people resisted the idea. After all, the college students would not have much money to donate to church projects and might not dress as well as the long-standing church members. After much prayer, the pastor prevailed and the outreach began.

Not long afterward the church was once again filled to overflowing every Sunday. Some of those who resisted the outreach still grumbled, but most of the congregation supported it wholeheartedly. One Sunday, however, the congregation's commitment was put to the test.

The service had already begun when a young man walked right down the center aisle and sat down cross-legged right in the aisle! He had obviously had a rough night. His hair and clothes were messed up and he did not smell as if he had bothered to shower. The pastor could hear the mumbling and felt as if his entire ministry was on the line. Just as he was about to say something to the young man, an old man stood up and, with the aid of his cane, began slowly walking down the aisle toward the young man. The pastor recognized him at once as one of the charter members who gave generously to the church. As usual, this old gentleman was dressed in his best suit. The pastor's heart trembled as he waited to see what would happen next.

When the old man had made his way down the aisle, he stood next to the young man, leaned on his cane, and slowly lowered himself to sit next to him. Together, young man and old man, they sat cross-legged, waiting to hear the pastor's message. To a hushed crowd the pastor said, "The sermon I have to preach doesn't compare to the message God has just given us."[1]

Types of Men's Groups

There are many different types of men's groups, but they can be broken down into two or three basic types. Each type has its own emphasis and focuses on various issues that men face. My own bias is toward twelve-step groups because the spiritual emphasis and the practicality of the twelve steps are hard to replace.

Alcoholics Anonymous

The twelve steps of Alcoholics Anonymous give the practical "how-tos" of experiencing God's grace by directing a person to take steps to relinquish control to God, steps of repentance, steps of forgiveness, steps to make amends, steps to maintain the disciplines of prayer and meditation, and so on. Emphasis in these groups is also placed on the natural outgrowth of sharing what God has done through people's recovery.

Men's Stag, Men's Only AA, OA, Al-Anon, Codependent's Anonymous, Sex/Love Addict's Anonymous, Gambler's Anonymous, Overcomers Outreach, etc.

Sobriety from an addiction, obsession with a person or compulsive behavior is an essential first step in recovery. Sadly, I have seen men who are not working a program of recovery from alcoholism, sexual addiction, eating disorders and so on begin to attend men's support groups. Because they are not actively working toward sobriety, these men only become more aware of how and why they are in addiction.

A man who is actively involved in a program of recovery from his addiction and is doing written step work is ready to face the deep hurt and grief he will feel as he heals from the wound of his father-son relationship. When that grief begins to surface, he will need other men in recovery from that particular addiction to be there for him so he doesn't fall back into the addiction. When addicted men who are beginning to face the father-son wound become involved in twelve-step programs, they can make substantial changes in their lives. The twelve-step groups provide the foundation of sobriety that enables men to face their woundedness.

Men's Ritual Groups

These men's groups follow the same principles as many twelve-step groups. No cross-talk is allowed, and each man has an opportunity to share. There is a time limit on sharing, but the group may drop the limit if a man is working through particularly deep grief or anger.

Men in these groups may pass a "talking stick" that helps to keep order in the group. The talking stick, which is decorated with feathers and fur, was used by Native Americans. It represents the fact that everyone is to listen to the man speaking and to respect that he is speaking from his heart. Only the man holding the stick may talk, and when he is finished, he passes the stick to the man next to him.

It would be interesting, in a church ritual group, to have each man who speaks hold the Bible. This would symbolize that God knows our hearts completely and that it is important for us to be totally honest in all that we say and do. This would also emphasize, to men who are Christians, the importance of their relationship with God and the need for honesty in their relationships with God and man.

A leader may be designated for this kind of group. He may open the meeting by sharing his own story, a poem, a passage from Scripture that illustrates an issue on which the group may focus or a fairy tale that has touched his life. The group may periodically conduct rituals or ceremonies when a group member feels the desire for an initiation ceremony connected to a life event, such as becoming a father, grandfather or husband. A topic such as shame might be selected as a theme for the group. The group may conduct a ritual for an individual man or the entire group to go through as a means of releasing or letting go of shame.

For information on men's ritual groups, contact Tracks in the Sand, P. O. Box 1828, Tustin, CA 92680, (714) 751–1012.

Men's Accountability Groups

I have worked with men who are involved in these small groups. Meeting weekly, these groups focus on particular themes, such as parenting, fidelity or honesty. The purpose of this type of group is to strengthen the commitment of men in the group to spend time with their families, to have trust, and so on.

Male Survivors of Sexual Abuse

As recovery plays a greater role in the Christian community and as men become more educated on men's issues, increasing numbers of men are coming forward to talk about past sexual abuse. It is estimated that as many as one in every six men has experienced sexual abuse. I believe that this number is low. As more change occurs within men, that number most likely will approach what it is for women: one in four.

A men's survivors' group focuses on the various types of sexual abuse that men experience. Sharing with other male survivors is a vital part of the healing process.

For information on these groups or how to form a group for male survivors of sexual abuse, contact : Virtues, Education and Support, P. O. Box 602, Brea, CA 92622–0602.

Discipleship and Bible Study Groups

I have included this category to clearly emphasize that the above groups are not substitutes for being in a relationship where men learn the disciplines of the faith. Developing the skills and tools of prayer and meditation on God's Word is the foundation on which men build and the manner by which they deepen their relationship with the Heavenly Father, His risen Son, and the fellowship of the Holy Spirit. The disciplines and tools for growing in our relationship with God can be integrated into any of the above-mentioned groups.

Format for a Men's Group

There is no perfect model for a men's group. This movement is in its infancy. As more men's groups develop and men share ideas, the strong Christian men's community that we all desire will develop. As men's groups develop in different churches, I would hope that representatives of all the groups will meet together and form a men's council, where new ideas and information can be shared and taken back to the other groups. It is important also that a men's group begin the ritual or initiatory processes that I have described in other parts of this book. This type of activity gives men's groups the life that is needed to help build a strong, functioning men's community. The potential for a strong men's community is exciting. Men's groups can be a key way to help activate men in the Christian community.

The following format is used for a men's group that meets under the auspices of the Single Parent's Ministry at First Evangelical Free Church in Fullerton, California. The format has been adapted to reflect changes that occur as men's groups change.

Leadership

Leadership within the group rotates from one meeting to the next, so all men learn to assume leadership. At the end of one meeting, the acting leader chooses the leader for the next meeting. The meeting time of the next meeting is determined by the group. Meetings vary in length from one to one and one-half hours. It is important for the acting leader to ensure that the meeting begins and ends on time. He is also responsible to enforce the guidelines of the meeting if group members begin to violate them. These guidelines provide a structure for the group, make it safe for men to share, and are the key to the group members' deepening in vulnerability from meeting to meeting.

The leader can use the following helpful phrases and ideas in conducting a men's group meeting:

Greeting—

"Hello, men. My name is _____, and I am a (recovering alcoholic, overeater, sexual addict, adult from a dysfunctional family, survivor of incest, work addict, and so on.) Welcome to the Men's Meeting.

"The purpose of this meeting is to give men a safe place to share—a place to learn who we are by sharing our feelings, desires, hurts, successes and goals in a real community of fellowship with other men. As we learn to share openly and honestly, and as we identify with others as they reveal themselves, we grow stronger as individuals, closer as a group, become clearer about our identities and what it is to be a man and develop a deeper, more real relationship with our own Father, God."

Group Rules—

"There are a few basic rules that we all need to follow in this meeting:

(1) When you share, first introduce yourself to the group by your first name and the particular issue you are strug-

gling with in your life, if you feel comfortable doing so. As an example, a man may say, 'Hi, my name is Bill, and I am a codependent.' The rest of the group then responds by saying, 'Hi, Bill.'

(2) When you are done sharing, the group will respond by clapping. This acknowledges the courage it takes to share.

(3) No cross-talk is allowed. No advice giving or fixing is allowed. When a man shares, no one is to interrupt or comment on his sharing. Go one by one around the group. If you do not feel like sharing, just say, 'I pass.'

(4) All sharing is done in the first person. We are to speak in the first person and share out of our own experiences and from our own feelings. Blaming others for our own problems keeps us from accepting responsibility for ourselves, our relationship with God and other men.

(5) This is an anonymous group. It is a sacred trust when one man shares with a group. Everything that is said in this group stays in this room.

(6) As men, we all carry some shame. Some of us carry more than others. We are to model Christ's love and acceptance by recognizing that we are all in different places in our spiritual, emotional and relational growth. These differences are essential to our group. We learn from those who are new in recovery and from those who have been in recovery for quite a while.

The group leader may then read the twelve steps of Alcoholics Anonymous*:

1. We admitted we were powerless over our dependencies— that our lives had become unmanageable.

2. Came to believe that a Power greater than ourselves could restore us to sanity.

3. Made a decision to turn our will and our lives over to the care of God as we understood Him.

4. Made a searching and fearless moral inventory of ourselves.
5. Admitted to God, to ourselves and to another human
   being the exact nature of our wrongs.
6. Were entirely ready to have God remove all these defects
   of character.
7. Humbly asked Him to remove our shortcomings.
8. Made a list of all persons we had harmed, and became
   willing to make amends to them all.
9. Made direct amends to such people wherever possible, except when to do so would injure them or others.
10. Continued to take personal inventory, and when we were
    wrong, promptly admitted it.
11. Sought through prayer and meditation to improve our
    conscious contact with God as we understood Him, pray-
    ing only for knowledge of His will for us and the power to
    carry that out.
12. Having had a spiritual awakening as the result of these
    steps, we tried to carry this message to alcoholics, and to
    practice these principles in all our affairs.
*   The Twelve Steps are reprinted with permission of Alco-
    holics Anonymous World Services, Incorporated. Permis-
    sion to reprint and adapt the Twelve Steps does not
    mean that A.A. has reviewed or approved the contents of
    any publication that reprints the Twelve Steps, nor that
    A.A. agrees with the views expressed therein. A.A. is a
    program of recovery from alcoholism. Use of the Twelve
    Steps in connection with programs which are patterned
    after A.A. but which address other problems does not
    imply otherwise.

Announcements—
(1) "There will be a five-minute break for coffee after the an-
    nouncements.

(2) So that everyone has a chance to share, please limit your sharing to ____ minutes." (Use this only if the group is large.)

(3) A group meeting is an opportunity to announce upcoming events. (For example, you might say, "On Saturday, we are meeting at Bill's cabin, where we will participate in an initiation ceremony for his son. His son has spent the past year preparing spiritually and emotionally to be welcomed into becoming a man."

Or you may say, "Thursday night, we are meeting at Bob's house. He is going to become a father for the first time, and we are going to participate in a ceremony where we share what we have experienced by being fathers and what God has taught us. Then we will have a ceremony through which Bill will be initiated into the role of fatherhood, to show that he is taking another step in his growth and maturity as a man. We want to support and share with him in this big step.")

Sharing Time—

"Our topic tonight will be _____." (The leader then chooses from a list of topics: shame, anger, loss/grief, sexuality, money, pride, alcoholism, lust, fatherhood, greed, humility, goals, prayer, rage, control, resentment, fear, or another topic that may meet the needs of the group.)

The leader then reads a Scripture verse, poem, etc., that is connected to the topic. He then shares his own feelings and struggles concerning the meeting's topic and asks if someone else would like to share. If no one volunteers, he can choose someone who will share. After the sharing is complete or it is time to end the meeting, the leader can read the following:

"In closing, let us remember that what we shared here is to remain within this room. The things that are said belong to the person who said them, and they are the person's own opinions. Take what you like and leave the rest. We are not to talk to outsiders about what someone else has said here. If we lose the integrity and confidentiality of the group, we lose the group."

The group leader may then close the group in prayer, with all the men joining hands and saying either the Lord's Prayer or the Serenity Prayer. The leader then talks to one of the men about leading the group during the next meeting.

Note: This particular group format models somewhat the format of a twelve-step meeting. I would like to thank Dan Nowak for sharing the material from his men's group. The material for the group format is an adaptation of the material his group uses.

Other resources for group formats include:

A Circle of Men: The Original Manual for Men's Support Groups by Bill Kauth (St. Martin's Press, 1992). This contains a week-by-week format for eight meetings. This particular group format allows for cross-talk.

The Overcomers Outreach *Freed* booklet and *Adults from Dysfunctional Families* group book also contain group formats that could be used for a men's group. These are patterned after the format of a twelve-step group.

Helpful Organizations

Overcomers Outreach, Inc.
2290 West Whittier Boulevard, Suite A/D
La Habra, CA 90631
(310)697–3994

Overcomers Outreach, Inc., is a nonprofit, Christ-centered ministry dedicated to helping anyone who would benefit from a twelve-step program. The organization also helps churches establish Christ-centered twelve-step support groups. As of this writing, there are now 1000 Overcomers Outreach groups in 47 states and 10 countries. Internationally, Overcomers Outreach is supported by the tax-deductible contributions of individuals who believe in its goals or have benefited from the program.

Overcomers Outreach is not intended to replace such twelve-step groups as A.A., Al-Anon, A.C.A., and so on. Rather, the organization seeks to supplement those programs and assist Christians who are in recovery. Overcomers Outreach views itself as a bridge between the twelve-step community and churches of all denominations. Its founders are Bob and Pauline Bartosh, who started the ministry based on their own recovery experience.

If you are interested in starting a Christian twelve-step support group in your church, contact Overcomers Outreach by phone or mail. Ask for *Freed,* a booklet available in English or Spanish that contains all the information you will need to conduct an Overcomers Outreach group. If an Overcomers Outreach group does begin in your area, please inform the central office so that people who call for information can be referred to your group.

Overcomers Outreach also has additional materials on recovery and starting recovery groups, which is available from the central office.

Other Twelve-Step Support Groups:

Adult Children of Alcoholics, Central Service Board
P.O. Box 35623
Los Angeles, CA 90035
(213) 464–4423

Alcoholics Anonymous
P.O. Box 459
Grand Central Station
New York, NY 10163
(212) 686–1100

Al-Anon/Alateen Family Group Headquarters
P.O. Box 182 Madison Square Station
New York, NY 10159
(800) 344–2666; (212) 302–7240

Debtors Anonymous
314 West 53rd Street
New York, NY 10018
(212) 969–0710

Emotions Anonymous
P.O. Box 4245
St. Paul, MN 55104
(612) 647–9712

Gamblers Anonymous
P.O. Box 17173
Los Angeles, CA 90017
(213) 386–8769

Incest Survivors Anonymous
P.O. Box 5613
Long Beach, CA 90800

Narcotics Anonymous, World Service Office
16155 Wyandotte Street
Van Nuys, CA 91406
(818) 780–3951

National Association for Children of Alcoholics
31582 Coast Highway, Suite B
South Laguna, CA 92677
(714) 499–3889

National Clearinghouse for Alcohol Information
P.O. Box 1908
Rockville, MD 20850

Overeaters Anonymous, World Service Office
2190 190th Street
Torrance, CA 90504
(213) 542–8363

Virtues—Victims of Incest Recover Through
Understanding, Education and Support
P.O. Box 602
Brea, CA 92622–0602

Sinners Anonymous
P.O. Box 26001
Austin, TX 78755–0001

Suggested Reading

Adams, Kenneth. *Silently Seduced*. Health Communications, Inc., 1989.

Alsdurf, James and Phyllis. *Battered into Submission*. InterVarsity Press, 1989.

Bly, Robert. *Iron John*. Addison-Wesley, 1990.

Carder, Dave; Henslin, Earl; Cloud, Henry; Townsend, John; Brawand, Alice. *Secrets of Your Family Tree: Healing for Adult Children of Dysfunctional Families*. Moody Press, 1991.

Cosby, Bill. *Fatherhood*. Dolphin Doubleday, 1986.

Dalbey, Gordon. *Father and Son: The Wound, The Healing, The Call to Manhood*. Thomas Nelson Publishers, 1992.

Dalbey, Gordon. *Healing the Masculine Soul*. Word Publishing, 1988.

Fisher, Robert. *The Knight in the Rusty Armor*. Wilshire Book Company, 1987.

Henslin, Earl. *The Way Out of the Wilderness*. Thomas Nelson Publishers, 1991.

Hicks, Robert. *Un-Easy Manhood*. Oliver Nelson, 1991.

Hunter, Mic. *Abused Boys*. Lexington Books, 1990.

Keyes, Ralph. *Sons on Fathers*. Harper Collins, 1991.

Levinson, Daniel. *The Seasons of a Man's Life*. Ballantine Books, 1978.

Liebman, Wayne. *Tending the Fire: The Ritual Men's Group*. Ally Press, 1991.

McClung, Floyd Jr. *The Father Heart of God*. Harvest House Publishers, 1985.

Miller, Keith. *A Hunger for Healing*. Harper Collins, 1992.

Osherson, Samuel. *Finding Our Fathers*. Ballantine Books, 1986.

Peale, Norman Vincent. *This Incredible Century*. Tyndale House Publishers, 1991.

Sheppard, Kay. *Food Addiction: The Body Knows*. Health Communications, Inc., 1989.

Smith, David. *Men Without Friends*. Thomas Nelson Publishers, 1990.

Sorenson, Amanda and Stephen, eds. *Time with God: The New Testament for Busy People*. Word Publishing, 1991.

Thompson, Keith, ed. *To Be A Man: In Search of the Deep Masculine*. Jeremy P. Tarcher, Inc., 1991.

Wilson-Schaef, Anne. *Escape from Intimacy*. Harper and Row, 1989.

ENDNOTES

Chapter One:

1. Rader, Dotson, "What Love Means," *Parade* (March 8, 1922): 4
2. Ibid., pg. 4
3. Watson, Thomas J. Jr. and Petre, Peter *Father, Son, & Co.* (New York: Bantam Books, 1991) pg. 288.
4. Bly, Robert, "Men's initiation rites" *Utne Reader*, (April/May 1986): 45.

Chapter Two:

1. Adams, Kenneth M. Ph. D. *Silently Seduced: When Parents Make Their Children Partners* (Deerfield Beach, Florida: Health Communications, Inc., 1992) pgs. 9-10.

Chapter Three:

1. Patterson , James and Kim, Peter, *The Day America Told the Truth: What People Really Believe About Everything that Really Matters* (New York , Prentice Hall Press, 1991) pg. 25.
2. Ibid., pgs. 25,26.
3. Ibid., edited statistics from throughout the book.
4. Covey, Stephen R., The Seven Habits of Highly Effective People: Powerful Lessons in Personal Change (New York: Simon & Shuster, 1989) pg. 18.
5. Ibid., pg. 18.
6. *Utne Reader,* April/May 1986. pg.44. This article written by Gail Early and originally appeared in the *Chico News and Review,* July 11, 1985.
7. Ibid., pg. 44.

Chapter Four:

1. Watson, Thomas J. Jr. and Petre, Peter *Father Son & Co.* (New York: Bantam Books, 1991) pgs. 366, 367.
2. Adapted from a story told by Robert Bly on the audio cassette *Fairy Tales for Men and Women*, available from Ally Press.

Chapter Five:

1. Watson, Thomas J. Jr. and Petre, Peter *Father, Son & Co.* (New York: Bantam Books, 1991) pg 288.

2. Osherson, Samuel *Finding Our Fathers* (New York: Fawcett Columbine, 1986) pgs. 54, 55.
3. From a survey of pastors from the Fuller Institute of Church Growth and reported to the Care Givers Forum in Colorado Springs, Colorado, November, 1991, as reported in the newsletter of life enrichment.

Chapter Six:

1. Arnold, Patrick M. *Wildmen, Warriors and Kings Masculine Spirituality in the Bible* (New York: Crossroad 1991) pg. 2.

Chapter Eight:

1. This is a recurring theme in Robert Moore's lectures and writings. Audio tapes of his lectures are available through the CC.G. Jung Institute of Chicago.

Chapter Nine:

1. Thompson, Keith, ed. *To be a Man in Search of the Deep Masculine* (New York: St. Martin's Press, 1991) pg. 52
2. Ibid., pg. 39
3. Ibid., pg. 37.
4. Ibid., pg. 43.

Chapter Ten:

1. Osherson, Samuel *Finding Our Fathers* (New York: Ballantine Books, 1986) pg. 53.
2. Clancy, Tom *Clear and Present Danger* (New York: G.P. Putnam's Sons, 1989) pgs. 490-492.
3. Osherson, Samuel *Finding Our Fathers* (New York: G.P. Putnam's Sons, 1989) pgs. 54.
4. Ibid., pg. 57.

Chapter Eleven:

1. Hicks, Bob *Uneasy Manhood* (Nashville, Tennessee: Oliver-Nelson Books, division of Thomas Nelson, Inc., 1991) pg. 45
2. Rosten, Leo *Rosten's Treasury of Jewish Quotations* (Northvale, New Jersey: Jason Aronson, Inc., 1988) pg. 239.
3. Walvoord, John F. and Zuck, Roy *The Bible Knowledge Commentary (Wheaton Illinois: Victor Books, 1985) pg 448.*
4. Ibid., pg. 448.

Chapter Twelve:

1. Adapted from a sermon of Pastor John Ridler of Bethany Reformed Church, Clara City, Minnesota, December 30, 1991.